19th Century Quotes *for* 21st Century Living

Anna Donovan and Ellen Ratner

Published by

Copyright © 2017 Anna Donovan and Ellen Ratner

Print ISBN: 978-0-692-88885-8

All rights reserved. No part of this publication may be reproduced, scanned, uploaded, stored in a retrieval system, or transmitted, in any form or by any means, electronic, mechanical, photocopying, recording, or otherwise, without the prior written permission of the publisher.

Edited by Shari Johnson
Cover & interior by TheBookCouple.com

Printed in the United States of America

*To my beloved grandchildren,
Emma, Arley, Annie and Jack.*
—Anna Donovan

*To Emmy Chetkin,
who has devoted her life to Spiritualism,
and to making Spiritualists feel at home.*
—Ellen Ratner

Contents

Introduction, 1

Judge John Worth Edmonds, 7
KNOWLEDGE AND WISDOM

Emma Hardinge Britten, 18
SPIRITUALISM

Dr. Valmour, 29
SKILL, TALENT AND
FULFILLMENT OF DUTY

Harriet Beecher Stowe, 35
COMMUNICATION AND WORDS

Fannie Buckner, 47
GRACE AND EMPATHY

Rebecca Jackson, 57
THE SOUL

Mary Todd Lincoln, 68
ADVERSITY

Victoria Claflin Woodhull, 75
WOMEN AND MEN

Sojourner Truth, 81
TRUTH AND LIVING WITH
YOURSELF

William Cooper Nell, 93
COURAGE

Jeremiah Carter, 97
HOME AND RELIGION

Horace Greeley, 112
ACCOMPLISHMENT AND
GOVERNING/GOVERNMENT

Frank Haddock, 124
CHARACTER

E.W. and M.H. Wallis, 135
LOVE

Cora Wilburn, 145
EXPERIENCE

Notes on the Sources Used, 149

Books Used for Quotations, 155

Acknowledgments, 157

Index, 163

About the Authors, 169

Introduction

As we were researching a topic on mental healing almost a quarter-century ago, we began to notice how rich and meaningful the Spiritualist quotes we were reading were to our current times—as relevant today as they were when written; most of them well over 125 years ago. Working individually, each of us gradually fell under the enlightened voices behind these messages, finding them to be a guiding force in our desire to turn difficulties and frustrations into positive efforts.

Knowing with absolute certainty the power in these beneficial and healing words, our enthusiasm piqued. In a simultaneous moment of inspiration, we turned to each other and expressed our desire to communicate these quotes to others.

Some of the quotes and messages are in direct opposition to each other, but then so much *is* in life.

The American social climate today is similar to that of the mid-19th century. Political, social, spiritual and emotional unrest has created a great need in many people to seek beyond traditional experiences for a fulfilling life in place of turmoil. At first glance, these often-labeled "new moments" appear to be provocative teachings and philosophies. A closer examination reveals them to be in line with early Spiritualist philosophy.

The Civil War is not directly addressed in these quotes, although some were written before, during and soon after the war. Spiritualists as a group were opposed to slavery, opposed to the death penalty, and were in favor of Women's Suffrage. Ann Braude has written the history of Spiritualists and Women's Suffrage in her book, *Radical Spirits, Spiritualism and Women's Rights in Nineteenth-Century America*. Free Love was also a cause of the Spiritualists, although it had to do with ownership and women's rights, and not as we might think of it now.

Encouraging the widespread popularity of this new religion in the 19th century was the fact that Spiritualist groups were small, intimate gatherings taking place in private homes. The context of these early years was an important factor in the attraction the movement had for women. Traditionally, women had found their greatest strengths within the context of their homes. When the Spiritualist movement entered their doors, it created a fertile ground for helping women enter public life in more substantial roles. Ann Braude chronicled this history in her book. It is not surprising then, that Spiritualism was one of the fastest growing movements in the mid-19th century. It provided a foundation of comfort for all who sought teaching and it has provided an ever-present link to the spiritual and social fabric of the Western world.

As we were reading the old Spiritualist newspapers, we began to understand more clearly the enduring presence Spiritualism has been in the history of American religious thought and social ideas. Although in the background, it has also had a profound influence on contemporary thought. It has provided an unshakable foundation of comfort for all who have sought its teachings. The early history of Alcoholics Anonymous was greatly influenced by Swedenborg, Home Circles, and Spiritualism. It has been a source of personal spiritual inspiration as well. Spiritualism played an integral role in the development of women's rights, African-American rights, and other reform movements in the mid-19th century. It provided early pioneers, especially women,

INTRODUCTION

with a platform for speech. It allowed those pioneers to take a role in leadership and to voice their opinions.

To the population as a whole, Spiritualism offered a very simple and comforting vision of life after death. It was, therefore, very compelling to those seeking faith at a time when rigid doctrines of the church were leaving followers disillusioned. The basic tenant of Spiritualism was the belief in continuous life. From the beginning, Spiritualists believed that people on earth were able to communicate with the spirit world and receive messages of guidance from them. These messages provided direction not only for the individual, but also for society as a whole. Spiritualists both then and now believe that the doorway to reformation is never closed to any human soul. Spiritualism teaches that the philosophy of right living applies to every aspect of everyday life and improves the lives of everyone.

While Spiritualism is known to have had its beginnings in a small town in upstate New York in 1848, there were earlier thinkers and believers who laid the groundwork for its emergence. Emmanuel Swedenborg, a scientist and philosopher living in Sweden in the 18th century, was the earliest modern western philosopher to formulate a concept of the spirit world. His investigations led to the development of the core Spiritualist belief that incarnate spirits can communicate with those who passed on. The Shakers, a community-oriented religious group founded by Mother Ann Lee in the 1770s, also preached a fundamental belief in the accessibility of the spirit world. In communicating with that world, the Shakers received inspirational songs and drawings as "gifts" from Spirit. These manifestations embodied the profound Shaker belief in each person's capacity to know and experience the Divine. The famous song "Simple Gifts" sung at President Clinton's first Inauguration was a Shaker "gift" song, said to be from Spirit.

These and similar influences helped shape the response to an extraordinary event that occurred in the town of Hydesville, New York, in March of 1848 at the home of John and Margaret Fox. It was the key event in the development of the Spiritualist religion. Inexplicable rapping noises or knockings began to occur on the walls of the Fox home. On Friday evening, March 31, 1848, the Fox children began imitating the raps. Determined to discover where they were from, the youngest Fox daughter began to communicate with the source by devising a system of knocks that represented the alphabet. A series of questions was asked and it was soon discovered that the raps belonged to the spirit of a peddler who had been killed in the house ten years previously. To help prove the validity of these knockings, neighbors of the Fox family were invited to ask their own questions of the spirit, all of which were answered correctly. Later, a partial skeleton was found that matched the rapper's description of himself. The news of the Hydesville rappings spread. It was referred to as a "spiritual telegraph," and many people began their own attempts to communicate with the spirit world.

Several months after the rappings first occurred, the Seneca Falls, New York, women's rights conference was held. This conference focused on the social, civil and religious rights for women. The very famous "Declaration of Sentiments" was written. Many of the women who were leaders at this conference were also early Spiritualists. Ann Braude reports that the table on which the Declaration of Sentiments was written had been visited by rappings when it was in the home of people who became Spiritualists.

It was not long before Spiritualist beliefs, the rights of women and the ending of slavery began to exercise their influence over American life. Harriet Beecher Stowe, one of the most widely read female authors of the 19th century, understood the public's interest in the new religion. She requested that her publisher send a copy of one of her books to a Spiritualist newspaper in order to get a print review.

Within a few years, there were by some counts over 200 Spiritualist newspapers disseminating news and Spiritualist philosophy in the English-speaking world. During the 1850s, there were very few American cities, towns or villages that did not have a local medium. The Spiritualist faith crossed religious, ethnic, and racial boundaries. In 1854, the Roman Catholic Church estimated that there were 11 million Spiritualists in America—nearly half the population (the 1850 census of the United States determined the population to be 23,191,876).

In the 19th century, Spiritualism helped give greater validity to ideas concerning social conditions. Its teachings encouraged people to take up the cause for the abolition of slavery, the abolition of the death penalty, and the care for the poor and the mentally ill. Rights of women and other minority groups were taken up by the Spiritualists as well. The commitment of Spiritualists to these issues and their ability to speak out in the face of strong opposition and protest are proof of the strength that Spiritualists received from their religion as well as the importance it held in the lives of its followers. It is no coincidence that the rise of Spiritualism in this country occurred during a period of great political and social unrest.

Many of the early Spiritualist pioneers or dabblers in communication with the dead were prominent figures of the 19th century. Victoria Woodhull, journalist and the first woman candidate for President of United States; author Harriet Beecher Stowe; Shaker Elder Rebecca Jackson; William Cooper Nell, who was an ardent abolitionist; and Sojourner Truth, author and tireless worker on behalf of oppressed and minority groups. These people and others investigated the teachings of Spiritualism.

Each section of this book contains brief biographies of someone who during the 19th century was either a self-proclaimed Spiritualist or one whose life was significantly influenced by the Spiritualist movement. The biography is followed by quotations that address a specific quality of that person. We feel that the quotes are an enlightening reflection on the lives and endeavors of these people, and we delight in sharing them with you.

We find it remarkable that these quotes, written over 100 years ago, are still applicable to our lives today. We need only to reach back into our history and pull these views forward to be inspired by them.

Some of the quotes were edited to reflect the language of our times. In other words, we edited the practice of referring to all people in the male gender. Some grammatical changes were made for clarification, and some quotes were edited for length. Writers in the 19th century were often quite verbose.

—Anna Donovan and Ellen Ratner

Judge John Worth Edmonds

John Edmonds was born into a prominent New York family in 1799. He was educated at Williams College and then Union College in Schenectady, New York. He read law and eventually entered the office of former President Martin Van Buren. He served in the state legislature and was a judge. His intellect and judicial powers enabled him to achieve outstanding success in public life.

Edmonds' excellent reputation served him well when in 1853 he was attacked by the press for his belief in Spiritualism. In 1851, he had been drawn toward Spiritualist ideas because he had been, in his own words, "withdrawn from society and depressed." He became preoccupied with death and the afterlife, and devoted two years to thoroughly investigating Spiritualism with all the diligence he applied to his public work.

Although his intention had been to expose the movement as a giant hoax, the conclusion he ultimately reached was just the opposite. He felt strongly that the knowledge he had gained would serve to help improve the lives of others as well. His belief in the healing powers of the Spiritual persuaded him to publicly acknowledge his viewpoints.

Some of the attacks on Judge Edmonds were particularly malicious. They ridiculed him for consulting his dead wife and other spirits when making decisions. They charged him as tantamount to a devil worshiper and tried to show evidence of his total abandonment of self-control. His defense of spiritual beliefs was called by the *New York Courier* "one of the most remarkable documents of the day." The paper found it hard to reconcile the profession of such beliefs with the rational, intellectual character of the Judge Edmonds the public knew and respected highly.

Edmonds' humanitarian instincts would lead him to the Spiritualist faith, but prior to that, he was recognized for his fair-mindedness and high moral principles in dealing with the social issues of the day. Because of this and his ability to humanize bureaucratic red tape, in 1836 President Jackson appointed Edmonds the official responsible for overseeing the implementation of the treaty between the United States and the Ottawa and Chippewa Indians. When he returned to New York, he was appointed inspector of Sing Sing Prison. At that time, New York prisons were considered corrupt, chaotic and fiscally mismanaged. Not only did Edmonds humanize punishment, but he also initiated a system of rewards for good conduct and founded an organization that helped released convicts establish an honest living.

Largely as a result of the controversy surrounding his religious belief, Edmonds resigned his seat on the court and focused his attention on Spiritualist pursuits. He became part of one of the first Spiritualist organizations in New York, "The Society for the Diffusion of Spiritual Knowledge." After committing many years to publishing and working for the Spiritualist Movement, Judge Edmonds returned to his highly respected practice of law.

JUDGE JOHN WORTH EDMONDS

Knowledge and Wisdom

Wise persons seek for the cause of the errors in themselves; fools, excusing themselves, seek for it in others.
—*The Banner of Light*,
June 1, 1861

What we need is not more colleges, but better ones—colleges in which our youth shall mainly be taught that which they most need to know, and which will make them signally useful to other people.
—Horace Greeley, quoted in
The Shekinah, 1852

Those who know their ignorance are the possessors of the rarest kind of valuable knowledge.
—*The Banner of Light*,
August 9, 1862

The intellect of the wise is like glass;
it admits the light and reflects it.
—THE BANNER OF LIGHT,
OCTOBER 15, 1898

People's greatest need is
knowledge of themselves.
—HENRY WOOD, IDEAL SUGGESTION
THROUGH MENTAL PHOTOGRAPHY, 1893

Ignorance is the cause of all discord. Those who know the truth should be patient and charitable with those who do not, remembering that they themselves were once in the darkness and saw not the light.
—JAMES J. OWEN,
SPIRITUAL FRAGMENTS 1890

To act is easy, to think is hard.
—THE RADICAL SPIRITUALIST,
JUNE 1858

JUDGE JOHN WORTH EDMONDS

A cat may look like the picture of innocence, but do not leave it alone with the canary.
—*The Banner of Light,*
July 23, 1870

Courage and composure come of knowledge and grow with it.
—*The Banner of Light,*
September 20, 1862

Pride is increased by ignorance; those who assume most know the least.
—*The Banner of Light,*
August 6, 1870

Read people as well as books; be sure to read yourself.
—*New England Spiritualist,*
August 30, 1856

Be temperate in diet; our first parents ate themselves out of house and home.
—THE BANNER OF LIGHT,
JULY 16, 1870

Those that can take advice are sometimes superior to those who can give it.
—A FOUNTAIN OF LIGHT,
VOL. 1, NO. 8, 1880

Many are intellectually great, but spiritually ignorant.
—THE WORLD'S ADVANCE-THOUGHT, NOVEMBER 4, 1890

Useful knowledge can have no enemies except the ignorant; it cherishes youth, delights the aged and is an ornament in prosperity.
—NEW ENGLAND SPIRITUALIST,
FEBRUARY 14, 1857

True education means more than the gaining of knowledge: it means also training of the body and the senses, and the best training of the mind and the heart.
—*The Temple Messenger*, September 1890

The body must be trained to obey the mind; the mind must be trained to give the body commands worth obeying.
—Annie Payson Call, *Power Through Repose*, 1891

What is a person without wisdom? They are like a ship without a rudder, liable to go astray at any time. Remember that selfishness leads without wisdom. Selfishness does not consult with wisdom.
—*The Voice of Angels*, January 2, 1878

Justice is a virtue of the mind; reward all people according to their worthiness.
—THE AGITATOR, JULY 1, 1858

It is not the quantity but the quality of knowledge that determines the mind's dignity.
—NEW ENGLAND SPIRITUALIST, APRIL 25, 1857

Any knowledge that is not internal consciousness as well as an external fact is no better than sunlight reflected from the moon.
—THE UNIVERCOELUM AND SPIRITUAL PHILOSOPHER, MARCH 3, 1849

No book is so full of beauty as the book of Nature, yet no book is so carelessly read.
—NEW ENGLAND SPIRITUALIST, AUGUST 9, 1856

JUDGE JOHN WORTH EDMONDS

> The best education is the one which best fits one for the duties, struggles and the enjoyments of life.
> —*The Temple Messenger*, September 1890

> There are two kinds of education. One is an acquisition of knowledge; the other is the development of wisdom.
> —*The Univercoelum and Spiritual Philosopher*, March 10, 1849

> Whatever increases the sum of human knowledge and augments the joys of the human soul is beneficial to the world.
> —Andrew Jackson Davis, *Penetralia: Being Harmonial Answers to Important Questions*, 1868

In the highest pursuit of truth, each mind must employ its own immortal reason.
—Andrew Jackson Davis, *The Temple: Concerning Diseases of the Brain and Nerves*, 1871

We have learned that wisdom is the blossom of pain, the fruit of suffering. We have found that if we live this life, we must try moral experiments and that we cannot go through life without doing many things that we regret.
—*The Banner of Light*, January 5, 1898

Seek wisdom and you will be sure to find her; but if you do not look for her, she will not look for you.
—*The Banner of Light*, May 28, 1857

Wisdom is a tree and active virtue its fruit.
—*The Banner of Light*,
August 6, 1870

There is nothing too sacred or too exalted
for the investigations of that soul whose
religious emotions and moral dignity
are inspired with the love of truth.
—Andrew Jackson Davis, *The Great
Harmonia: The Seer* vol. 3, 1853

Anything is too holy for an angry debate, but
nothing is too sacred for calm investigation.
—Andrew Jackson Davis, *The Philosophy
of Special Providences: A Vision*, 1851

Thought is the wind, knowledge is
the sail, humankind is the vessel.
—*The Banner of Light*, July 12, 1862

Emma Hardinge Britten

Emma Hardinge Britten is considered the mother of Modern Spiritualism and the earliest historian of the Spiritualist movement. She was born in London in 1793, and began earning money by teaching music at the age of twelve. She came to America to pursue a career as an actress and performed briefly in a play in New York. During this same time, she continued her connection to music by composing under the pseudonym, Ernest Reinhold.

While in New York, Emma was invited to a séance. Due to her evangelical upbringing, even though she had been having mediumistic experiences since her childhood, she left the first séance aghast at what she had witnessed. Shortly thereafter, she was persuaded to attend another séance where the medium presented Emma with evidence that she could not possibly have known. Discovering that she possessed great talent as a medium, Emma Hardinge Britten began "sitting." In one séance she delivered a message about a ship, "The Pacific," that had gone down at sea. Although the owners of the ship accused her of saying things that were not true, the ship was never heard from again. This was the same ship on which she had journeyed to America.

Although saddened by this experience, she was nonetheless even more confident in her powers as a medium.

Increasing her contact with Spiritualists, Emma continued to give music lessons and séances. In addition, she was a prolific writer and began delivering inspirational lectures. Despite suffering from rheumatism and chest and throat ailments, she traveled the country giving speeches on Spiritualism. She insisted that Spiritualism was a new religion based on facts and supported by science, saying that Spiritualism was "a religion separate in all respects from any existing sect."

Spiritualism

The man or woman who lives from within and seeks to spiritualize every department of being is the true spiritualist.
—The Banner of Light,
October 15, 1898

Inharmony attacks the weakest part of the spiritual nature, as disease attacks the weakest organs of the body.
—The World's Advance-Thought,
no. 3, 1890

A true Spiritual philosophy can no more ignore political questions than it can the laws of physical health.
—Friends of Progress,
November 1864

Let in a ray of light at the upper window.
—*The Radical Spiritualist*,
May 1859

When Socrates was told by a friend that his judge had sentenced him to death he answered, "And has not nature passed the same sentence upon them?"
—*The Banner of Light*,
August 1, 1870

Our physical wants increase as we sink into materialism. They decrease as we rise spiritually.
—*The Universal Republic*,
no. 9, 1890

True Spiritualists, of all people, should be fraternal with one another. The universe is the result of the fraternization of forces.
—*The Banner of Light*,
August 6, 1870

The spiritual nature does not grow in noise, but in quiet, not in society, but in solitude.
—THE BANNER OF LIGHT,
MARCH 14, 1863

There are far more shriveled souls from too great worldly prosperity than from too little.
—THE WORLD'S ADVANCE-THOUGHT,
NO. 3, 1890

The wise, the just, the pious, the brave, live in their death and flourish in the grave.
—JOSEPH GREEN AS QUOTED IN LIFE THOUGHTS FROM PULPITS AND FROM POETS, ALFRED I. HOLMES, 1872

Sir Walter Scott on his deathbed, "I feel as if I were myself again."
—AS QUOTED IN THE SPIRITUAL CLARION

People can reach the earth with their senses,
but only with their ascending thoughts
can they attain the spiritual realm.
—The Universal Republic,
no. 9, 1890

We need not look to tables moved by unseen hands, nor to sounds from invisible causes, nor to wonderful words from entranced mediums, nor to all or any of these things; or behold the manifestations of spirit presence, or to the phenomena of Spiritualism. No, not to these. Every breath we breathe, every motion of our bodies, is a tangible manifestation of an indisputable evidence and presence of an immortal spirit. There is nothing from the minutest atom to the highest seraph a mind can conceive, that is not a medium for the transmission of spiritual truth from a world of intelligent spiritual life.
—The Banner of Light,
June 11, 1857

Our eyes are here to set on earth and earthly things; look heavenward a little more, and you will not only see more of Heaven yourself, but encourage others to do the same. Heaven is more of a condition than a place; you need not wait for death to take you there. If you reach out for it, it will come to you.
—*The Harbinger of Light*, December 3, 1889

The seeker after truth . . . should be aware of his or her imagination and keep it under the steady control of reason. Many are self-deceived and think they voice the thoughts of wise spirits.
—*The Banner of Light*, September 17, 1900

The divine Spirit is an educator—
it will guide you into all truth.
—Henry Wood, *Ideal Suggestion Thorough Mental Photography*, 1893

The purpose of Spiritualism is and has been . . . To spiritualize humankind, we must permit the influence of the soul to throw around us the x-ray of spiritual truth through which we may be led to find the source of spirituality and truly know ourselves.
—*The Banner of Light*, September 17, 1857

Every person of reason and intuition knows that God is in the deepest heart—an inexhaustible fountain of love as well as of wisdom—expanding through all that illimitable structure that we call the physical universe.
—Andrew Jackson Davis, *Free Thoughts Concerning Religion: or Nature Versus Theology*, c.1872

We go to the grave of a friend saying "a person is dead" but angels throng upon the person saying, "a person is born."
—*The Agitator*, July 1858

You who would learn the truth should go to the most secret chamber of your own soul. The spirit of God lives there. There you should go to pray, to sing, to commune with your guardian spirits.
—Andrew Jackson Davis, *The Great Harmonia: The Seer*, vol. 3, 1853

Spiritualism is in everything that surrounds us; the wisdom, the goodness and the love of God. God smiles in every sunbeam and even the clouds are but the shadow of God's great protective hand . . . Theology sees the devil in all things. Every sunbeam is suspected of having a fiendish origin. Every cloud is a punishment for Adam and Eve's transgression . . .
—*The Banner of Light*, May 28, 1857

A person must fall back on themselves and begin the work of purification of their own heart.
—*The Banner of Light*, quoted from Ralph Waldo Emerson, September 17, 1857

> To the spiritually minded, all realities are clothed in a glowing divinity; everyday occurrences are miraculous.
> —Andrew Jackson Davis, *The Great Harmonia: The Seer*, vol. 3, 1853

> The law and method of the spiritual culture require the following: Be contented with the past and with all it has brought to you. Be thankful for the present and for all you have. Be patient for the future and for all it promises to bring you.
> —Andrew Jackson Davis, *The Great Harmonia: The Teacher*, vol. 2, 1875

> The human body was made to develop the human spirit.
> —Andrew Jackson Davis, *The Great Harmonia: The Physician*, vol. 1, 1855

To be like God let us aspire to God.
—ANDREW JACKSON DAVIS, THE GREAT
HARMONIA: THE TEACHER, VOL. 2, 1875

The Spirit is the wine procured from the vintage of the Universe. It is obtained from the ultimate ethers of all elements combined.
—ANDREW JACKSON DAVIS, THE GREAT
HARMONIA: THE THINKER, VOL. 5, 1883

No circle [home circle] where brotherly or sisterly love was excluded ever obtained any spiritual developments.
—THE BANNER OF LIGHT,
APRIL 22, 1859

Dr. Valmour

Dr. Valmour was an African-Creole whose real name was John B. Aversion. He was a freed person, and a blacksmith in New Orleans. The amazing story of Dr. Valmour is that he was walking by a building where Emma Hardinge Britten was lecturing when, it has been described, John B. Aversion was "seized" and entered the building. Emma Hardinge Britten immediately saw his abilities and said to the entire lecture hall, "Let the Brother come up here to me and give me strength to speak. He is full of electricity." According to reports, he sat on stage for the next two hours.

He began public séances but was forced by the police to discontinue them. According to historian Melissa Daggett, one local clergy member sent the police to his blacksmith shop because he was jealous of him.

He was known after that as a healer and as one of the main members of a regular séance sitting known as the Cercle Harmonique. This group was remarkable in that they kept diligent séance records. There were individual messages, and most of the focus from the spirit world was about forming a society that focused on justice. The messages were usually in French. One historian, Emily Suzanne Clark, author of *A Luminous Brotherhood: Afro-Creole Spiritualism in Nineteenth-Century New Orleans* said that the séances allowed participants to interact with people they normally would not have been in touch with.

Dr. Valmour died in February 1869 after the Civil War, but continued to be part of the circle by giving continual messages. During his lifetime, he conducted healing at his home where he also ran his blacksmith shop. One member of the Cercle Harmonique compared him to Jesus. He is known to have cured a bishop from Italy who had visited prominent doctors in Europe, but no one could restore his voice. Dr. Valmour cured him, and quite quickly.

After he passed to spirit, he delivered this message to the Cercle Harmonique: "Don't cry . . . my spirit is carefully being lifted towards beautiful regions . . . a magnificent and grandiose panorama of the eternal life is unfolding . . . Valmour is triumphant. Oh! My brothers, continue to combat the error, the injustice and the superstition, and you will have the satisfaction of the heart."

Skill, Talent and Fulfillment of Duty

Everyone has a mission to fulfill: it is a high and lofty one, though it might not be what some are aspiring for.
—*New England Spiritualist,*
June 30, 1855

Attention is the duty we owe others; cleanliness is what we owe ourselves.
—*The Banner of Light,*
July 6, 1870

There is pleasure in contemplating good, there is great pleasure in receiving good. But, the greatest pleasure of all is in doing good.
—*A Fountain of Light,*
vol. 1, no. 9, 1880

The keys of a piano are arranged so that when struck by a mastermind, beautiful peals of music resound. But let the same keys be struck by an unskilled hand and what discord proceeds.
—A FOUNDATION OF LIGHT,
VOL. 1, NO. 2, 1880

Never despise humble services; when large ships run aground, little ships may pull them off.
—THE SPIRIT MESSENGER,
FEBRUARY 19, 1853

No sense as valuable as that which is called common; and it is also the most uncommon.
—THE BANNER OF LIGHT,
MARCH 5, 1880

Seek to know yourself, what you are and what you can do, and aim within your reach.
—FROM A LECTURE BY HUDSON TUTTLE,
QUOTED IN THE AGITATOR, JANUARY 1, 1850

DR. VALMOUR

Confidence is a plant of slow growth.
—The Agitator,
October 15, 1858

We cannot think alike, we cannot work alike, nor is it necessary that we should. Let each, then, in their own peculiar way, work on in the manner in which their nature and their education have best fitted them to work.
—A Fountain of Light,
vol.1, no. 6, 1870

Every talent is spontaneous. The one adapted to yourself you may cultivate, but not another's. And be your talent dull and unpromising, remember that what is well and nobly done is "pure gold." There is as much need of the delicate flower, as the gigantic oak, the wind and the rain as the gentle sun. It requires this great diversity to form the complete system in nature.
—A Fountain of Light,
vol.1, no. 4, 1880

Employment begets cheerfulness.
—*The Banner of Light*,
July 30, 1870

Life is sometimes as a smooth flowing river, again as the raging ocean; sometimes we gently glide, others we battle with the fierce waves. But be it rough or smooth waters, we still move on.
—*Foundation of Light*, vol. 21, 1881

A spare and simple diet contributes to the prolongation of life.
—*The Univercoelum and Spiritual Philosopher*, January 20, 1849

Who never walks save where they see a person's tracks makes no discoveries.
—J.G. Holland quoted in *A Fountain of Light*, vol.1, no. 20, 1881

Harriet Beecher Stowe

One of the best-known women writers of the nineteenth century, Harriet Beecher Stowe is best remembered for her work, *Uncle Tom's Cabin*. In much of her writings, which include poems, stories, and novels, she exhibits a curiosity about psychic phenomena. There is some evidence that in 1844 she and her brother Reverend Henry Ward Beecher conducted mesmeric (hypnotic) experiments. When the Spiritualist movement came to light and was spreading across the country, she, like others, became very curious. The ties to the Spiritualist movement were all around her. Her half-sister Isabella Beecher Hooker was a devoted Spiritualist and her husband, Calvin Stowe, was an untrained medium who spoke to Harriet about his psychic experiences in his early childhood.

She later used her husband's story as a model for a visionary boy in a story. When her son Henry drowned in 1857, she consulted with mediums while publicly denouncing any result from these contacts. She continued her private investigations from her mediumistic contacts.

She wrote to Elizabeth Barrett Browning about receiving messages from her departed son. She contributed articles on

Spiritualism to her own newspaper, *The Christian Union,* as well as to other publications at the time. She often wrote about Spiritualism to her friends and continued to be influenced by its teachings. In one letter to Oliver Wendell Holmes she wrote: "I remember a remark you once made on Spiritualism . . . You spoke of it as modifying the sharper angles of Calvinistic belief, as a fog does those of a landscape. I would like to talk with you some on Spiritualism and show you a collection of very curious facts I have acquired . . ." Using her own writing as a form of communication, Harriet was able to explore the religion of Spiritualism. A close reading of her writing reveals them to be spiced with ideas and suggestions of this belief.

Communication and Words

Resolve to study the art of keeping your mouth shut. It is a fine art, a very fine art, and few there be that learn it.
—*The Banner of Light,*
October 15, 1898

There is poetry in nature. It glitters in the wave, the rainbow and the stars; its softer tones go sweetly up from the thousand-voiced harp of the wind.
—*The Spirit Messenger,*
January 4, 1851

There is babbling more than enough, but little true speech.
—*The Radical Spiritualist,* 1860

Keep your temper in disputes.
The cool manner fashions the red-
hot iron into any shape needed.
—*The Banner of Light*,
April 11, 1887

You may imprison the wind, you may chain the
lightening, but you cannot bind the free thought
and free utterance of a nation of free people.
—*The Spirit Messenger*,
December 18, 1852

Poetry is only born after painful journeys
into vast regions of thought.
—*The Radical Spiritualist*,
November 1859

Words are but the shadows of ideas, while
ideas may be imperishable entities.
—*Spiritual Telegraph*,
May 22, 1852

People seldom improve when they have no better model than themselves to copy after.
—*The Banner of Light*,
May 11, 1861

The dreamers do not stop dreaming . . . The dream may be false and foolish—nine dreams in ten are so. But the hope of the world lies in the great tenth dream.
—*The Banner of Light*,
October 8, 1898

Slanders issuing from beautiful lips are like spiders crawling from the blushing heart of a rose.
—*The Banner of Light*,
July 5, 1862

Silence is a cheap virtue.
—*The Radical Spiritualist*,
September 1858

Gossip and malice usually travel in company.
You should hesitate before you decide
to entertain one of them as a guest.
—*The Banner of Light*,
November 12, 1898

The slanderer, unfortunately, is like the wasp
and not the honeybee. They generally do
not lose their sting with the first use of it.
—*The Banner of Light*,
August 29, 1865

Every great poem is in itself limited by necessity,
but its suggestions are unlimited and infinite.
—*The Banner of Light*,
April 30, 1857

A rich imagination will discover and reveal new beauties. It will not prevent or obscure its meaning.
—*The Banner of Light*,
September 1, 1900

A majority of humankind can love their neighbors far better at a distance than they can close at hand.
—*The Banner of Light*,
October 8, 1898

Idealists and poets elevate their race.
—*The Radical Spiritualist*,
June 1858

Cheerfully acknowledge merit in others, and in return you will always receive the kind consideration that you desire.
—*The Banner of Light*,
April 25, 1857

Never condemn your neighbor unheard, however many the accusations against him; every story has two ways of being told. Justice requires that you hear the defense as well as the accusation.
—*The Banner of Light*,
November 13, 1858

We are born with two eyes
but with one tongue,
in order that we should see
twice as much as say.
—*The Banner of Light*,
September 25, 1858 and October 15, 1898

Those who tell the faults of others intend to tell others of your faults.
—*The Banner of Light*,
September 25, 1858

Blame no person for what they cannot help. We must not expect of the dial to tell us the hour after the sun has set.
—*The Banner of Light*,
May 28, 1857

The cure of an evil tongue must be done at the heart.
—*The Banner of Light*,
June 7, 1862

A torn jacket is soon mended, but hard words bruise the heart of the child.
—*The Banner of Light*,
April 8, 1857

Give me the poetry, inspiration of life, and you may have the rest.
—*The Radical Spiritualist*,
October 1859

A young woman ought, like an angel, to pardon the faults she cannot comprehend; and an elderly woman, like a saint, because she has endured trials.
—*The Banner of Light*,
May 7, 1859

True glory is said to be doing what deserves to be written, writing what deserves to be read, thinking what is fit to be spoken at all times, and speaking words that flow only from a true and generous heart.
—*The Banner of Light*,
May 24, 1862

If you want to know a woman's true character, linger after the guests are gone and hear what she says of them.
—*The Banner of Light*,
November 30, 1861

Life is short; and that portion of it that one human being devotes to injuring, punishing and destroying another will pay but a poor dividend on the final settlement of differences.
—*The Banner of Light*,
April 30, 1857

Have you spoken ill of your neighbor? What would you have said or done had you been in your neighbor's place?
—*The Banner of Light*,
November 5, 1898

Kinder is the looking glass than the wine glass, for the former reveals our defects to ourselves only; the latter to our friends.
—*The Banner of Light*,
April 23, 1859

The *Uncle Tom's Cabin* of white slavery—prostitution—has yet to be written.
—The Radical Spiritualist,
October 1859

Loquacious mouths are like badly managed banks. They make large issues on no solid capital.
—The Banner of Light,
June 11, 1859

Healthy criticism is the best mental fertilizer because it plows up the soil of thought and prepares it for the best seed-grains of truth.
—Andrew Jackson Davis
in *Answers to Questions*

Fannie Buckner

In 1913 at the age of 42, Fannie Buckner became the first woman minister ordained in the state of West Virginia. The Church where she was a minister is now known as the First Spiritualist Church, Way Memorial Temple, and had its 100th Anniversary in 2001. Not only was she a woman, she was African-American as well. Her first work was as a teacher in Maryland and West Virginia.

Rev. Buckner, according to her granddaughter, always financed Christmas for her family, and did so as if she were rich.

Her granddaughter says that Rev. Buckner gave spirit messages from an Indian Chief named Sonto. She also gave spirit messages from a German man named Crenshaw. Her voice would change from her own to the entity she was bringing to people.

Many prominent people from the community, both black and white, attended her church services. She was also known for doing private spirit readings as well as healing. She was loved and revered by many in her community—an example of grace and empathy.

She had a stroke at the age of 65, just a few hours after saying she did not feel well.

[We are grateful to Sue-Beth Warren for her research on Rev. Buckner.]

Grace and Empathy

A great person will not trample upon
a work nor cringe to an emperor.
—*The Radical Spiritualist,*
January 1860

Ridicule is but a gross pleasure—too
rough an entertainment for those who
are highly polished and refined.
—*The Banner of Light,*
July 5, 1862

Sympathy creeps from one soul to another.
It answers the cry of the wounded
heart a great many miles distant.
—*The Banner of Light,*
April 25, 1857

Little drops of rain brighten meadows and little acts of kindness brighten the world.
—Quoting author Alice Carey in *New England Spiritualist*, August 1, 1856

The heart that is not touched with pity at another's failings and weaknesses, as well as their misfortunes, has only learned one-half the lesson of humanity. Kindness is the only true educator for a soul.
—James J. Owen, *Spiritual Fragments* 1890

Gratitude is the memory of the heart.
—*The Banner of Light*, September 20, 1862

Learn to know all, but keep thyself unknown.
—*The Agitator*, vol.8, 1891

Generous and self-denying efforts are
not in vain, but are painted on the
eternal world and never effaced.
—L.H. Grindon quoted in A Fountain
of Light, vol.1, no. 2, 1880

Let none of us seal our lips until freedom,
justice and equality pervade all hearts.
—The Radical Spiritualist,
May 1858

We may concede any person a right without
doing a person wrong; but we can favor
no one without injuring someone.
—The Agitator,
August 15, 1858

There are many graceless preachers on
grace, many uncharitable ones on charity.
—The Banner of Light,
June 21, 1862

Large souls are never envious or jealous—they never seek to build themselves up by pulling others down. They delight in the success and good luck of their neighbors, and they are glad when others are made glad, even though their own pathway may be beset with trouble. When fortune smiles upon their lives, they are always ready to share it with their friends and neighbors.
—James J. Owen,
Spiritual Fragments, 1890

The act of giving to others opens our own soul in spiritual exercise, and we become receptive only in proportion to our willingness to impart.
—The Spiritual Clarion,
August 18, 1857

By doing good with their money, people stamp the image of God on it.
—The Banner of Light,
July 30, 1870

He or she is looked upon with fear and
distrust and regarded as an anarchist,
a reckless iconoclast, or social brigand,
because he or she wishes to build
something better for the common good.
—*The Banner of Light*,
April 25, 1857

True charity does not require us to smile at
vice and wink at sin; it does demand that we
make a distinction between sin and the sinner.
—*The Banner of Light*,
April 25, 1857

If we could read the secret history of our enemies,
we should find in each person's life sorrow
and suffering enough to disarm all hostility.
—*The Banner of Light*,
April 25, 1857

Many people who drop a tear at the sight of distress would be better to drop a sixpence.
—The Radical Spiritualist,
December 1859

A generous mind does not feel as belonging to itself alone, but to the whole human race.
—Friends of Progress,
November 1864

The more wine a person drinks,
the more they whine.
—The Banner of Light,
July 23, 1859

If a person never relieves distress, or feels for others' woes, how can that person look for the smiles of Providence to rest upon themselves? How can they ask for blessings when they have never bestowed any?
—The Banner of Light,
May 29, 1858

Use yourself to kindness and compassion
and you may expect kindness
and compassion in return.
—THE BANNER OF LIGHT,
MAY 28, 1857

To commit a falsehood is like the cut
of a saber; the wound may heal, but
the scar of it will remain forever.
—THE BANNER OF LIGHT,
APRIL 11, 1857

Perfect happiness for an individual is
impossible while anything suffers.
—THE UNIVERSAL REPUBLIC,
NO. 9, 1890

The future is not only before
us, it is also above us.
—THE BANNER OF LIGHT,
NOVEMBER 5, 1898

We open the hearts of others
when we open our own.
—The Radical Spiritualist,
January 1860

A philosopher resembles a cucumber—
when most cut up, is perfectly cool.
—The Banner of Light,
April 23, 1859

Let us halt and watch and listen
and see what we shall gain.
—Annie Payson Call,
Power Through Repose, 1891

We pray that our hearts many never
become closed against sympathy for
those who are afflicted with poverty.
—The Spiritual Clarion,
May 30, 1857

Never trust a person whom you have seen able and willing to deceive another; they will deceive you should the opportunity arise.
—The Banner of Light,
August 20, 1857

To see Athens, one must have Athenian eyes.
—The Agitator,
vol. 8, 1891

In peace, justice is of some effect, but in war the innocent and the guilty suffer alike.
—The Banner of Light,
June 15, 1861

Rebecca Jackson

Rebecca Cox Jackson was born just outside of Philadelphia in 1795. She was a free black woman, worked as a seamstress, and lived a very settled life caring for her family after her mother and grandmother died. She was taken in by her brother who was at that time a minister.

It was not until she was thirty-five that her life took on a very different trajectory. She had a profound religious experience, one that she described as a religious awakening. It happened during a thunderstorm. She had always been very frightened of thunderstorms and in the midst of this one, when she prayed for either "death or redemption" she experienced a message of "peace, joy and consolation."

She felt it was an awakening of her soul to the message and calling of God. She believed her mission was to spread the word of God and to let others experience the same healing that she had received. She prayed to be able to read the Bible, and later wrote: "I picked up my Bible, ran upstairs, opened it, and kneeled down with it pressed to my breast, prayed earnestly to Almighty God if it was consisting to His holy will, to learn me to read His holy word. And when I looked on the word, I began to read. And when I found I was reading, I was frightened—then I could not read one word. I closed my eyes again in prayer and then opened my eyes and began to read. So I done, until I read the chapter."

Rebecca started experiencing dreams and spiritual gifts, such as healing. She became interested in Spiritualism and trained herself as a Medium. She was known to have read Judge Edmond's book on Spiritualism. She said she was able to reach spirits and communicate with them through séances held in her home. Spirits, it is said, asked to speak through Rebecca. She held prayer meetings in homes, and they were attended by white people as well as blacks. She moved from a private, stable existence into a very public career—first as a preacher, and then later as a founder of a Black Shaker Community. One biographer described her close relationship with Rebecca Perot as her protégé and companion, but we don't know anything more about the relationship of the two women. As Shakers, they were not permitted any form of sexual relationship. After Rebecca Jackson died, Rebecca Perot took on her name as "Mother Rebecca Jackson."

Rebecca Cox Jackson's religious beliefs and her commitment to helping others understand their own worth were similar to those held by Spiritualists, especially in teaching others the value of their own soul.

The Soul

Out of truth and goodness comes the beautiful, which ever seeks to adorn the soul with the wondrous garlands of love.
—*The Banner of Light,*
April 11, 1857

Real glory springs from the silent conquest of ourselves.
—*The Banner of Light,*
July 9, 1859

Age dims the luster of the eyes and pales the roses on beauty's cheeks . . .but dim as the eye is and frail and feeble that once strong and erect body, the immortal soul may look out through these failed windows and feed day by day on that love [of] God [to] human kind that lifts us and makes us akin to angels.
—*The Banner of Light,*
May 8, 1857

Deep down in the innermost recesses of the soul lingers a dim consciousness of something outside of the physical being that is real selfhood.
—The Banner of Light,
May 15, 1858

Mighty truths lie in the soul, which bring peace and happiness when found.
—The Harbinger of Light,
October 1, 1870

The person that seeks for the highest and best in their own life, is sure to find it.
— James J. Owen,
Spiritual Fragments, 1890

I am alarmed when I have walked a mile in the woods bodily without getting there in spirit.
—The Banner of Light,
September 8, 1900

Care not for the material things in a selfish way
above your material needs; the advanced
soul can make no use of them.
—The World's Advance-Thought,
no. 3, 1890

Intuition is the light of the human soul.
—The Spirit Messenger,
January 1, 1853

Life. Carlyle says that each person carries
under their hat a "private theater,"
beginning and ending in eternity.
—The Banner of Light,
August 13, 1857

Thought is prayer; it is the exercise
of the soul and the deeper it is the truer . . .
if the thoughts are above, the soul is above;
if below, the soul is there also.
—The Banner of Light,
May 12, 1858

We lie in the lap of immense intelligence,
which makes us receivers of its truth
and organs of its activity.
—The Banner of Light,
September 3, 1857

Solitude bears the same relation to the mind
that sleep does to the body. It affords the
necessary opportunities for repose and recovery.
—The Banner of Light,
April 3, 1858

Prayer is the soul's sincere desire unuttered
or unexpressed. It may exist unexpressed.
—The Banner of Light,
July 30, 1857

The normal mind dwells in the present, the more awakened mind dwells in the eternal.
—Katharine Newcomb, *Helps to Right Living*, 1899

Nothing is apparent to ordinary vision until it is painted upon the window of the soul.
—William Denton and Elizabeth M.F. Denton, *The Soul Of Things; or, Psychometric Researches and Discoveries*, 1871

The divine soul is the parent of the human soul, both eternal.
—*The Spirit Messenger*, November 27, 1852

The deepest sorrows lie unseen within the silent chambers of the soul.
—*The Spiritual Clarion*, January 14, 1818

Creation is a beautiful sermon, terminating with a grand, glorious conclusion.
—Andrew Jackson Davis,
The Soul

The end of all prayer is that the soul shall go forth in harmony with the eternal goodness.
—*The Temple Messenger*,
September 1880

In sleep we sometimes wander through the soul's picture gallery, and catch glimpses of its beauty; but of its grandeur and perfection we have not even dreamed.
—William Denton and Elizabeth M.F. Denton, *The Soul of Things; or Psychometric Researches and Discoveries*

The outward person perishes, but the inward person is renewed every day.
> —THE BANNER OF LIGHT,
> SEPTEMBER 20, 1862

The disease of the soul is folly, of which there are two kinds—ignorance and madness.
> —THE FOUNTAIN OF LIGHT,
> VOL. 1, NO. 3, 1881

Power comes to the individual through its sympathy with the community of souls.
> —HERALD OF PROGRESS,
> MAY 1861

The kingdom of heaven is within you and conscience is the divinity that rules therein.
> —ANDREW JACKSON DAVIS, THE GREAT HARMONIA: THE PHYSICIAN, VOL. 1, 1855

The soul and body are as strings of musical instruments, set exactly at one height—if one is touched, the other trembles. They laugh and cry and are sick and well together.
—*The Agitator*,
August 1, 1858

The human soul is a spark of divine intelligence, a germ of eternal life; like a seed sown in the earth, it germinates and grows and it expands and unfolds.
—*The Banner of Light*,
May 15, 1858

There is a spiritual atmosphere within the material atmosphere. The soul feeds on the one, the body upon the other, until by a refining process, they blend into one, whereby the spirit is made to increase in substance.
—Andrew Jackson Davis, *The Great Harmonia: The Reformer*, vol. 4, 1857

If every person would endeavor to know themselves as a Soul-being, the lessons of houses, lives and events would soon be revealed to all.
—The Banner of Light,
September 8, 1900

Life is light and shadow—sunshine and storm.
—The Banner of Light,
August 9, 1862

I must contain, as soul, all that God is in quality, in order to become conscious of God in the smallest degree.... Self is all that you understand. It is all you will ever know, for in understanding the self, you know the Infinite.
—Katharine Newcomb, Helps to Right Living, 1899

Mary Todd Lincoln

One would hardly consider a First Lady of the United States to be someone associated with adversity. However, Mary Todd Lincoln was exactly that person. She was born to wealth and her family actually owned slaves. Her mother died when she was six years old and the relationship with her stepmother was not a good one. Later, she lived with her sister in Illinois and dated Lincoln's adversary, Stephen Douglas. She had four sons with President Lincoln; one died before Lincoln became president, one died in the White House, and one died in 1871. Only one son survived her.

Mary Todd Lincoln supported her husband in his views on slavery, even though several of her siblings worked or fought for the Confederacy. While Lincoln was president, she attended séances at a house in Georgetown. Nellie Colburn, a medium, claims that Mrs. Lincoln brought President Lincoln to one of them. There is some debate as to whether Lincoln attended séances conducted by medium John Conklin in The White House. The séances were said to have taken place in the Red Room.

In her years as First Lady, Mary Todd Lincoln was accused

of overspending in the redecoration of the White House. She was present when her husband was shot at Ford's Theatre, and after President Lincoln's death she saw a Spiritualist photographer who produced a photograph of Lincoln. Many think the photograph is a forgery.

In today's diagnostic terms, she might be thought to have had bipolar disorder, although there are physicians who think she had pernicious anemia. When she was about to jump out of a window because of a fire that did not exist, her son had her committed to an asylum. However there is some debate that he committed her for her belief in Spiritualism.

She was eventually able to leave the asylum, but things were never the same for her. After receiving help from an attorney and fellow Spiritualist, she was able to live with her sister as well as travel in France. She died at her sister's home in Illinois at the age of 63.

Adversity

The lessons of sorrow: Some hearts, like primroses, open most beautifully in the shadows of life.
—*The Banner of Light*,
April 11, 1875

Many of the waves of trouble, like those of the ocean, will, if we await them calmly, break at our feet and disappear.
—*The Banner of Light*,
April 28, 1864

Life's disappointments! What bitter tears they cause to gush forth from the depths of sorrowing souls. Sometimes they come so thick and fast they embitter one against the world; sometimes they act as spurs to the one that they come to.
—*The Banner of Light*,
October 22, 1898

Every heart has its secret sorrow, which the world knows naught; and oftentimes we call a person cold, when they are only sad.
—Reprinted from the poems
of George W. Light,
The Banner of Light, April 18, 1857

Troubles are like babies, they grow bigger by nursing.
—The Banner of Light,
May 21, 1859

A full heart is as difficult to carry as a full cup; the least thing upsets it.
—The Agitator,
June 1, 1858

A person cannot judge pleasure, who has never tasted pain.
—The Banner of Light,
April 3, 1858

19th Century Quotes for 21st Century Living

Why speak of age in a mournful strain?
It is beautiful, honorable and eloquent.
Welcome the snow of age for it is
the emblem of peace and rest.
—The Philosophical Journal/
The Religio-Philosophical
Journal, October 14, 1865

As the brilliant colors with which the
forests are arrayed in October and caused
by the sting of frost, so some of the loveliest
and brightest virtues that adorn humanity
are caused by the sting of affliction.
—The Banner of Light,
April 9, 1859

The pebbles in our path weary us, and make
us sore-footed, more than the rocks that
only require a bold effort to surmount.
—The Banner of Light,
August 13, 1857

Although the deed may be the same,
there is an excuse for impulse,
but not for deliberate evil.
—*The Fountain of Light*,
vol.1, no. 3, 1880

A smooth sea never made a skillful mariner, neither do uninterrupted prosperity and success qualify for usefulness and happiness. The storms of adversity, like those of the ocean, excite the intention, skill, and fortitude of the voyager.
—*The Banner of Light*,
August 13, 1857

A wise person ought to hope for the best, be prepared for the worst, and bear with equanimity whatever might happen.
—*The Banner of Light*,
April 25, 1857

Every picture has its light and shade, every life its happiness and misfortune; the two combine to form a beautiful contrast, to make a perfect whole. Day breaks, matures into noon, then deepens into night—which is the most beautiful?
—THE BANNER OF LIGHT,
APRIL 10, 1858

Those who are forever fretting and grieving because of some disappointment or seeming defeat may find, if they examined themselves, that it was far better for their higher natures that they missed the coveted position or treasure.
—THE BANNER OF LIGHT,
OCTOBER 22, 1998

Were life all happiness we should not know how to prize it; were it all trouble, we could not survive it; but the latter makes us brave, and strong to endure.
—THE BANNER OF LIGHT,
APRIL 10, 1858

Victoria Claflin Woodhull

The infamous Victoria Woodhull began her life in poverty in Homer, Ohio. She was born in 1838 as the daughter of an alleged arsonist, Ruben Buckman, and a Spiritualist named Roxanna Claflin. Victoria Woodhull claimed to have had her first visions at the age of three, and by the age of ten she said she had been visited by her familiar spirit, Demosthenes. Victoria's sister, Tennessee Celeste, was quick to recognize her sister's gifts as a medium, and along with their brother they created a traveling show featuring Victoria demonstrating her abilities. Victoria was only fifteen when she married Dr. Canning Woodhull. Their marriage produced two children, but ended in divorce eleven years later. Woodhull continued traveling with her sister and her partner, sometimes billed as her husband, James H. Blood.

In 1868, the two sisters were comfortably installed in Manhattan—in part because of the generous friendship of the wealthy, and with support from Spiritualist Cornelius Vanderbilt. He helped Woodhull and her sister start a successful brokerage business. During this same time, through his financial investment and the sisters' ventures, the women founded a journal, *Woodhull and Claflin's Weekly.* This was an important mouthpiece for what was considered Woodhull's radical ideas on women's rights and social reform. These ideas were influenced by the freethinking ideas of the Spiritualist movement.

Through their numerous books and pamphlets, Woodhull and her sister disseminated their ideas on reforming society and government. Among the most controversial were changes that Victoria Woodhull advocated in the relationships of men and women and family. She believed that those relationships should not be based on the ideas of ownership of the wife, but rather on the importance of the quality of the sexes, and what was known at the time as "free love." Her involvement in social and governmental issues as well as her exceptional abilities as a public speaker led her to organize the "Equal Rights Party." She was the first woman to run for president of the United States; however, her first selected running mate, Frederick Douglass, chose not to run.

The reform efforts ended in scandal and Woodhull and her sister finally settled in England in 1877. It was there that Victoria was married for the third and final time to the wealthy banker John B. Martin. Her final years were spent performing charitable works, lecturing, writing and traveling. Although some would say that she lived a sedate married life at the time, she never gave up all of her radical ideas. She wrote several books and with her daughter edited the magazine, *The Humanitarian.* She returned to the United States occasionally, but remained living in England until her death in 1927 at the age of 89.

Women and Men

Though men boast of holding the reins,
the women in general tell them
which way they must drive.
—*The Banner of Light*,
June 15, 1861

Man would be hard and unpolished
granite but for woman.
—*The Banner of Light*,
April 30, 1857

The last word is the most dangerous of machines. Husband and wife should no more strive to get it than they would struggle for possession of a lighted bombshell. Married people should study each other's weak points as skaters look for the weak part of the ice in order to keep off them.
—*The Banner of Light*,
April 9, 1859

According to Milton, Eve kept silent in Eden to hear her husband talk. "Alas," said a gentleman recently, "there have been no Eve's since." "Because," a lady quickly retorted, "there have been no husbands worth listening to."
—The Banner of Light,
March 12, 1880

Women will inevitably develop the world.
—Andrew Jackson Davis, The Great Harmonia: The Teacher, vol. 2, 1875

It is an old and true saying that a man should not marry unless he can support a wife; we are beginning to doubt seriously whether a woman can prudently marry unless she can support a husband.
—The Banner of Light, February 7, 1863

The love that has ends will have an end.
—The Banner of Light,
April 27, 1861

> . . . the harmonious proportions of humanity's future structure will depend entirely upon the education and elevation of the female master-builders.
> —Andrew Jackson Davis, *The Great Harmonia: The Teacher*, vol. 2, 1875

> Woman wields the great Archimedean lever, whose fulcrum is childhood, whose length is all time, whose weight is the world, whose sweep is eternity.
> —Andrew Jackson Davis, *The Great Harmonia: The Reformer*, vol. 4, 1855

> There is nothing in a true marriage that authorizes one partner to tyrannize over the conscience of the other. Where this is attempted it may be well that the usurpers, whether male or female, should learn the lesson of respect for the rights of others. When once learned, he or she will bless God for every pang it has cost.
> —*The Banner of Light*, May 11, 1861

Woman is the ladder by which we
climb from earth to heaven.
—The Banner of Light,
April 30, 1857

In the mouth of many men, soft words
are like roses that soldiers put into the
muzzles of their muskets on holidays.
—The Banner of Light,
April 18, 1857

Woman is indeed a bright, a beautiful
creature. Where she is, there is paradise;
where she is not, there is a desert.
—The Banner of Light,
April 30, 1857

Woman is the comforter and supporter
of man under his cares and misfortunes,
and the bitter blasts of adversity.
—The Banner of Light,
April 30, 1857

SOJOURNER TRUTH

Sojourner Truth was born in Ulster County, New York, in approximately 1797. Born into slavery, she won her freedom before New York State abolished slavery in 1827. She then moved to New York City. In June of 1843, Sojourner Truth embarked on the start of what she considered her God-given religious mission to be a voice for change among minority and oppressed groups. She dropped her given name of Isabella Baumfree and took the name she felt God had instructed her to take—Sojourner Truth. She devoted the rest of her life to traveling the country, promoting rights for African-Americans and women.

Sojourner Truth spoke at the National Spiritualist's Convention in 1868. Whether she became a Spiritualist or not, her faith was based on the fundamental principle of Spiritualists: the Golden Rule. "Do unto others as you would have them do unto you." Her empathy for the oppressed and her steadfast pursuit of universal equality made for gifts of vision that seemed to come from a higher realm.

She felt there could be no individual commitment to God until people first made a commitment to their fellow human beings. Stressing the importance of people making deeper connections, she felt there could be a noteworthy society. She once asked during a lecture, "How can you expect to do good to God unless you first do good to others?" She was described as having a vision of the world that was truly spiritual, as well as having a gift. She said, "I'm speaking words that came from the heart." Her teachings correlated with those of early Spiritualists who advocated for the rights of the oppressed.

As a political activist, Sojourner Truth worked as a Union spy and traveled with the troops to inspire black enlistees with her stories and spirituals. Her activities took her to Washington, D.C., to meet President Lincoln in 1864. To her surprise, she discovered that President Lincoln not only knew her name, but also knew about her heroic efforts during the Civil War. In her later life she served on the Freedman's Bureau to petition Congress for money to help former slaves in their new lives. Believing that they would find greater freedom and opportunities elsewhere, she encouraged newly freed men and women to move west. Sojourner Truth's fight for equality and justice continued her entire life, never diminishing even as she grew old. She once said, "I am above eighty years old; it is about time for me to get going. I have been forty years a slave and forty years free and would be here forty more to have equal rights for all." Her dedication to a life lived according to principle inspired countless others who followed the call of justice.

Truth and Living with Yourself

That person is richest who strives to make the soul the reflector of that which is good and true. Out of truth and goodness comes the beautiful, which ever seeks to adorn the soul with the wondrous garlands of love.

—The Banner of Light,
April 11, 1857

Conscience, be it ever so little a worm while we live, grows suddenly to a serpent on the deathbed.

—The Banner of Light,
March 7, 1863

Nature is a kind and gentle mother to all who live in harmony with her laws, and who obey her mandates.

—James J. Owen,
Spiritual Fragments, 1890

Motion in the human body is like music is an art. We should move as if every muscle strikes a note, so that only harmony results.
—Annie Payson Call,
Power Through Repose, 1891

The most disagreeable situation for a person is to be unable to reconcile their heart and conduct.
—*The Spiritual Clarion*, May 9, 1857, and
The Banner of Light, September 17, 1857

Every parent is like a looking glass for their children to dress themselves. Parents should care to keep the glass bright and clear.
—*The Banner of Light*,
January 29, 1870

Always back your friends
and face your enemies.
—*The Banner of Light*,
February 14, 1863

When we discern justice, when we
discern truth, we do nothing by ourselves
but allow a passage to its beams.
—Ralph Waldo Emerson quoted in *The Banner of Light*, September 3, 1857

Let us not fret ourselves with extravagant desires.
—*The Banner of Light*,
January 8, 1870

The person who loves truth with all
of their heart will love those who
suffer for the sake of the truth.
—*The Banner of Light*,
July 16, 1870

To be good is to be happy. Angels are happier than humans, because they're better.
—Alfred I. Holmes, *Life Thoughts From Pulpits and From Poets*, 1872

The rich might buy good cigars, but the poor might do a better thing by not smoking at all.
—*The Banner of Light*, January 8, 1870

God made people a "living soul" and therefor people are a soul, not just having a soul.
—Henry Wood, *Ideal Suggestion Through Mental Photography*, 1893

Labor to keep alive in your breast that little spark of celestial fire, Conscience.
—George Washington as quoted in *The Banner of Light*, April 20, 1851

Riches got by deceit cheat no person as much as the getter.
—*The Banner of Light*, March 19, 1880

It takes a good many shovels full
of earth to bury the truth.
—The Radical Spiritualist,
December 1859

And quietness of mind is also
essential to interior light.
—Andrew Jackson Davis, The Great
Harmonia: The Physician, vol.1, 1855

Sin is worse in the eye, worse in
the tongue, worse still in the heart,
and worst of all in the life.
—The Banner of Light,
August 6, 1870

There is something beautiful in a serene
and happy old age. To the man or
woman who has lived their best, old age
brings joy and not sadness. Whoever
does their best can do no more.
—James J. Owen,
Spiritual Fragments, 1890

Labor performed solely in the interests of self, without regard to the end in view, debases every person who undertakes it. Every action should be spiritualized.
—THE BANNER OF LIGHT, DECEMBER 17, 1898

For physical happiness, obey the physical laws; for organic happiness, obey the organic laws; for moral happiness, obey the moral laws.
—ANDREW JACKSON DAVIS, THE GREAT HARMONIA: THE SEER, VOL.3, 1853

Truth overcomes falsehood, and suspicion cannot live before perfect frankness.
—THE UNIVERCOELUM AND SPIRITUAL PHILOSOPHER, JANUARY 20, 1849

The surest way of imparting heavenly truths to others is by letting those truths shine brightly in our lives.
—NEW ENGLAND SPIRITUALIST. OCTOBER 11, 1856

If mortals would avoid the pain and suffering, they must grow wise and good in soul by using every moment to some advantage for the good of those that need aid, and for the love of good.
—*The Banner of Light*,
November 20, 1858

Error is mortal and cannot live.
Truth is immortal and cannot die.
—Andrew Jackson Davis as quoted in
The Radical Spiritualist, September 1858

True Christianity never made a person a slave; it is bigotry that does this.
—*The Radical Spiritualist*,
May 1858

Faith and science meet and harmonize in one great system of universal truth.
—*The Shekinah*, 1852

Truth wears no mask, bows at no human shrine, seeks neither place nor applause; she only asks a hearing.
—A heading on *The Philosophical Journal/ The Religio-Philosophical Journal*

One noble life, or a single noble deed, sets up conspicuous in the sight of all [and] becomes a fountain of life to many.
—*The Banner of Light,* April 11, 1857

Contentment is a pearl of great price, and whoever procures it at the expense of ten thousand desires, makes a wise purchase.
—*The Banner of Light,* June 25, 1870

Only what a person does, and what they continue to do, and persist in doing can a person show character.
—*New England Spiritualist,* December 8, 1855

Never defend an error because you once thought it to be the truth.
—*The Radical Spiritualist,*
November 1858

Nine years before he died, when verging on the grave, Sidney Smith said one of the evils of old age was thinking every illness is the beginning of the end. When a person expects to be arrested, every knock at the door is an alarm.
—*The Agitator,*
August 15, 1858

A person's outer government is an exact counterpart to their inner government. The strongest desires in them become their ruler.
—*The World's Advance-Thought,*
no. 3, 1890

Live selfishly for yourself and you will sit down at the end of life dissatisfied with human existence.
—Andrew Jackson Davis,
Philosophy of Spiritualism

There is no more useful person on this earth, no nobler character than the truth-seeker.
—*The Harbinger of Light*,
August 1, 1874

Truths not understood do people no good.
—*New England Spiritualist*,
June 30, 1855

Strive by willpower and inward growth to live less in bondage to circumstances.
—Andrew Jackson Davis, *History and Philosophy of Evil* 1858

Those who labor for humankind, without care for themselves, have already begun their immortality.
—*The Banner of Light*,
May 28, 1858

WILLIAM COOPER NELL

William Cooper Nell was born in 1816. He devoted his life to establishing equal rights for African-Americans. As a child he suffered an act of prejudice, the memory of which served throughout his life as a guiding force in his crusade. Having been denied, solely because of his color, the academic prize from his Boston grammar school that he rightly deserved, it inspired him to work throughout his life for equal rights of all children, regardless of color. As a young man, Nell was moved by what he read in *The Liberator,* the abolitionist paper published by William Lloyd Garrison, a devoted Spiritualist who believed that Spiritualism would be a voice for abolition. Neil and Garrison developed a lifelong friendship that gave mutual support to their common causes. Spiritualist philosophy gave Nell much of his strength as an energetic advocate for human rights. Among his earliest experiences were the séances he held with the Fox sisters. He also knew prominent Spiritualists of his time.

Nell studied law in the Boston office of William I. Bowditch. He chose not to apply for admission to the bar, feeling that the required support for the Constitution of the United States was in conflict with his commitment to abolishing slavery. Instead, following his Spiritualist leanings, he actively joined the anti-slavery and equal rights movement. In 1840, believing strongly in the liberating effect of education and with the memory of his childhood slight still very much alive, Nell put his name at the head of the list of the first petition submitted to the Massachusetts legislature asking that all public schools be open to black children. Long years of his devotion to educational reform contributed significantly to the desegregation of Massachusetts public schools in 1855. Nell also played a major role in the Underground Railroad and as an ardent opponent of the Fugitive Slave Act.

Nell's passionate devotion to more than one cause took its toll on his health, and in 1851 he was forced to retire temporarily from his many causes. Not content to be idle, he kept his commitment by being a journalist and author. Through his association with *The Liberator*, Nell had met Frederick Douglass in the 1840s, and he became publisher of Douglass's anti-slavery newspaper, *The North Star*. At the same time, he wrote pamphlets on African-American history. He was a major force in the struggle to allow African-Americans to serve in the military in the Civil War. In 1861, the Postmaster of Boston ignored the restrictions on hiring blacks and appointed Nell as Clerk in the postal service, the first African American to hold a federal post.

Living according to his own words, Nell was increasingly optimistic. He understood clearly that it was through courageous perseverance that African-Americans would gain the position of equality that was inherently theirs.

Courage

If you would not have affliction visit you twice,
listen at once to what it teaches.
—*The Banner of Light*,
September 17, 1857

A wise man ought to hope for the best
and be prepared for the worst.
—*The Banner of Light*,
April 25, 1857

We need more independence of soul . . .
Courage enough to do the bidding
of our instincts and rebuke the
wrong that timidity generates.
—Andrew Jackson Davis, *The Harmonial Man*, 1872

Each human soul is identical in germ.
There is no essential difference between people.
—Andrew Jackson Davis, *The Great Harmonia: The Reformer*, vol. 4, 1855

If a sailor should turn back every time they encounter a head wind, they would never make the voyage. One who permits oneself to be baffled by adverse circumstances will never make headway in the voyage of life.
—*The Banner of Light*, August 13, 1857

Jeremiah Carter

Jeremiah Carter founded what is now called Lily Dale, the world's largest community devoted to the religion of Spiritualism. He lived in Leona, New York, and was physically "enfeebled." A mesmerist (hypnotist) from Vermont was invited to lecture, but had to leave Leona before he could treat Jeremiah Carter.

Using techniques learned from the mesmerists, Jeremiah Carter began to heal. He did this while in a mesmeric state and while in this state, a spirit named Dr. Hedges spoke to the people who were gathered around him. Mesmerism (Hypnotism) and like experiments were held at a yearly picnic on Cassadaga Lake. In 1877, Spirit voices asked Jeremiah Carter to begin a camp meeting there, and it became a home for the religion of Spiritualism.

Carter was constantly asked by people who wanted healing to speak with the spirit entity, Dr. Hedges. A Dr. Hedges did exist, but he had passed to Spirit in 1848. Jeremiah Carter did not charge, or only charged fifty cents, to all that came to him for healing.

The Lily Dale camp meeting began in 1879, and was the start of what is now known as Lily Dale. The land was purchased for $1845. Dr. Carter, as Jeremiah Carter was called, passed to Spirit in 1897 at the age of 83.

Home and Religion

Get a home, rich or poor, get a home and learn to love that home. Make it happy by your beaming presence; learn to love simple pleasures, flowers of God's own planting and music of your own—the bird, wind, waterfall. So shall you help to stem the tide of desolation, poverty and despair that comes upon so many through scorn of little things. Oh, the charm of a little home! Comforts dwell there that sun the guided halls of society. Live humble in your little home, and look to God for a grander one!
—*Banner of Light*,
April 3, 1858

To the true person the world is hallowed ground, and all seasons holy.
—*The Radical Spiritualist*,
October 1859

Teach your children to love: to love the rose, the robin, to love their parents, to love their God. Religion is love— love to God, love to other humans.
—*The Spirit Messenger*,
December 18, 1858

There is not an obscure home among the mountains where the whole romance of life, from its dawn to its setting, through its brightness and gloom, is not lived through.
—*New England Spiritualist*,
August 9, 1856

A firm faith is one of the best divinities, a good life is the best philosophy, a clear conscience the best law, honesty the only true politic.
—*The Banner of Light*,
January 8, 1870

Divine Greatness is reflected in all things.
—ANDREW JACKSON DAVIS, *THE GREAT HARMONIA: THE TEACHER*, VOL. 2, 1875

The person who saves their smiles and kind words for their neighbors and bestows nothing but affronts and abuse on the spouse and child has not yet learned the alphabet of life.
—JAMES J. OWEN, *SPIRITUAL FRAGMENTS*, 1890

The universe is to be regarded as a complete whole, yet each part is perfect in itself, and every part reflects the glory of the creator.
—*THE SPIRIT MESSENGER*, OCTOBER 18, 1852

Heaven is holy happiness. Happiness comes from higher development. Higher development comes from holy aspirations.
—*THE FRIEND OF PROGRESS*, MAY 1865

Prayer may not make the Deity more willing to give, but makes the supplicant more worthy to receive.
—*The Spiritual Clarion,*
June 30, 1857

Religion is not the specialty of any one feeling, but the mood and harmony of the whole of them. It is the whole soul marching heavenward to the music of joy and love.
—*The Banner of Light,*
January 1, 1870

A new bud is put on the tree of time.
—*The Spirit Messenger,*
January 1, 1853

Churches are not empty when their pulpits are occupied by men and women who can stir hearts and instruct minds of the people.
—*The Golden Way,*
March 1891

People are not saved according to how they die, but according to how they live.
—*A Fountain of Light*,
vol. 1, no. 6, 1880

Do we love to be at home because there we can rule and fret, and find fault without restraint, and devote ourselves to our own pleasure; or because there we reciprocate all kindly affections and help to fill out the harmony of a happy household?
—*A Fountain of Light*,
vol. 1, no. 2, 1880

The worst way to reform the world is to condemn it.
—*The Radical Spiritualist*, 1858

To the spiritually minded, all realities are clothed in a glowing divinity; everyday occurrences are miraculous.
—Andrew Jackson Davis, *The Great Harmonia: The Seer*, vol. 3, 1853

You cannot build a Temple for the Spirit of Holiness to dwell in out of stone and mortar; it must be built on the soul, after the true model and the foundation-rock of love, mercy and justice toward humanity. An edifice of earth without a tremor.
—*A Foundation of Light*, vol. 1, no. 3

We are all building a soul-house for eternity, yet with different architecture.
—Henry Ward Beecher as quoted in *Friends of Progress*, November 1864

My country is the universe, my home
the world, my religion to do good.
—The Philosophical Journal/
The Religio-Philosophical
Journal, October 7, 1865

All formations have a portion of
God in their structure.
—Kingdom of Heaven,
January 1874

Everybody embodies themselves in their
works, and we find in their religious life
the autobiography of their inward being.
—The Shekinah, 1852

The lonely mountain, the desolate
wilderness and the tempestuous sea are
all consecrated by the holy Presence.
—The Shekinah, 1852

JEREMIAH CARTER

The religious world is wary of the
husks of creed and dogma.
—*Free Thought Magazine*, 1896

Every mind is a lens, so to speak, on which
the sun and earth paint new pictures.
—Andrew Jackson Davis,
The Present Age and Inner Life, 1853

Heaven is near to those hearts
that seek its presence.
—*The Spirit Messenger*,
October 30, 1852

Genius hath its triumphs, fame its glories,
wealth its splendor, success its bright
rewards, but heart only hath its home. Home
only! A true home is more than the world,
more than honor, and pride and fortune—
more than all earthy things can give.
—*The Banner of Light*,
May 28, 1857

The earth is my footstool. To do good is my mission. Nature is my golden rule, my God and my religion.
— *Free Thought Magazine*,
March 1900

How can a person ask for blessings when they have never bestowed any?
— *The Banner of Light*,
May 29, 1858

In "Treasury of Thought" we read: Religion is universal; theology is exclusive. Religion is humanitarian; theology is sectarian. Religion united humankind; theology divided it. Religion is love; theology preaches love and practices bigotry. Religion looks to the moral worth of people; theology to their creed. Religion is peace; theology is the apple of discord.
— *Free Thought Magazine*,
February 1896

Which is more sublimely the word of God, that which God has written in God's own hand on every blade of grass, on every bud and leaf, in every flower's cup, in every bird, beast and insect, or that which the hand of humans have inscribed in a Bible, Koran or Veda?
—*The Agitator*,
November 15, 1858

To willing minds the Infinite always speaks. Boundless Justice is the highest manifestation of true religion.
—Andrew Jackson Davis, *History and Philosophy of Evil*, 1858

There is a spiritual atmosphere within the material atmosphere. The soul feeds on one, the body upon the other, until by a refining process, they blend into one, whereby the spirit is made to increase in substance.
—Andrew Jackson Davis, *The Great Harmonia: The Reformer*, vol. 4, 1855

A religion that does not bind its followers together for good and noble purposes is a serious menace to the well-being of society.
—The Banner of Light,
April 9, 1889

There is nothing too free, too stupendous, too magnificent, or too holy for human consumption.
—Andrew Jackson Davis, The Great Harmonia: The Teacher, vol. 2, 1875

So many sects, so many creeds
So many paths that wind and wind
When just the art of being kind
Is all the sad earth needs
Ella Wheeler Wilcox,
Free Thought Magazine, March 1900

Order is heaven's first law.
—The Shekinah, 1852

Life is a journey, and they only who have traveled a considerable way in it are fit to direct those who are just setting out.
—*The Banner of Light*,
July 12, 1862

Happy are they who, because of harmony and freedom of Soul, cannot depart from home.
—Andrew Jackson Davis,
The Great Harmonia

A person of words and not of deeds,
is like a garden full of weeds.
—*The Banner of Light*,
April 3, 1858

Decision and character will often give an inferior mind command over a superior.
—*The Banner of Light*,
September 29, 1900

It is always best to do one's duty, even though foolish, inconsiderate ones are ready to curse and slander you for it. The wound of the gossip and slander is always the deepest.
—*The Banner of Light*,
November 12, 1898

Progress is the wand of divinity.
—*The Spiritual Clarion*,
January 14, 1860

No person has a right to do as they please, except when they please to do right.
—*The Banner of Light*,
May 11, 1861

Charity begins at home,
but does not end there.
—*A Fountain of Light*,
vol. 1, no. 9, 1880

Jealousy beats the very opposite of what it seeks. It stands in its own light, and casts an evil shadow on all around. Cast it out and put love, charity and patience in its place.
—*The Banner of Light*,
November 17, 1900

A clear conscience is sometimes sold for money, but is never bought with it.
—*The Banner of Light*,
May 29, 1859

Horace Greeley

In City Hall Park, New York City, there is a statue of Horace Greeley that was dedicated in 1916. It proclaims him as the founder of the *New York Tribune*. However, there is far more to his life than his memorial statue.

Horace Greeley was born in New Hampshire in 1811, the oldest of five children. He learned to read before he was five years old, and although he was offered a scholarship to a private school that had an excellent reputation, his parents were too proud to accept it.

He left home when he was a teenager, seeking to earn a living as a printing apprentice. He was 15 years old when he was apprenticed to a printer of a newspaper in Vermont. Four years later he went to Erie, Pennsylvania, and worked for *The Erie Gazette*.

In 1834, he became editor of *The New Yorker* magazine. While there, his opposition to slavery, as well as the government's exploitation of the American Indian, became known. He founded a daily newspaper in 1841, the *New York Tribune*, which was in existence until 1966.

Although most scholars do not think he invented the famous phrase "Go West, young man, go West," he frequently gave that advice in person and in print. "If any young man is about to commence in the world with little in his circumstances to prepossess him in favor of one section above another, we say to him publicly and privately, 'Go to the West; there your capacities are sure to be appreciated and your industry and energy rewarded.'"

Greeley and his wife had seven children, but only two of them lived to adulthood. When a son died in 1849, the Greeley's offered a room to the two Fox sisters, who led séances in their home. The Greeleys even offered to pay for one of the Fox sister's education. Although Horace Greeley later declared Spiritualism a swindle, at one point an editor wrote up the results of a séance in the *New York Tribune*.

Horace Greeley served in Congress very briefly and ran for President in 1872, where he lost in a major way. The Electoral Vote was 286–66. His wife died before the election and he died shortly after the election.

He was considered a journalist, a politician and a Spiritualist.

Accomplishment and Governing/Government

God gives people opportunities only.
—*The Radical Spiritualist*, 1858

It is far better to be educated to a life of usefulness, no matter how humble, and earn your way through the world, than to carry a diploma in your pocket and live on your friends.
—James. J. Owen,
Spiritual Fragments, 1890

Some frauds succeed from the apparent candor, the open confidence, and the full blaze of ingenuousness that is thrown around them.
—*The Carrier Dove*,
August 8, 1891

Every person can really be great if
they trust their own instincts.
—The Radical Spiritualist,
August 1858

Practice flows from principle: as a
person thinks so will they act.
—The Friend of Progress,
December 1864

When will the world learn that there are higher
and better uses for human energies than in their
exclusive devotion to acquisition of wealth?
—James J. Owen,
Spiritual Fragments, 1890

Faultfinding does not require and does
not indicate a higher order of talent.
—The Banner of Light,
March 19, 1870

Turn not to the past; the present
is better and more powerful.
—*New England Spiritualist*,
June 18, 1857

Most people work for the present, a few work
for the future, the wise work for both.
—*New England Spiritualist*,
June 18, 1857

Art is long, judgement difficult,
opportunity transient.
—*The Radical Spiritualist*,
October 1860

A ruler who appoints a person to office
when there is another person more qualified
for it, sins against God and the State.
—*The Banner of Light*,
December 7, 1870

Peace and war alike originate in the heart.
—Friends of Progress,
December 1864

There is a resistless fascination in a person who is well balanced and wholesome.
—Andrew Jackson Davis,
The Genesis and Ethics of Conjugal Love, 1874

Thought, discipline, and control is the key that unlocks spiritual storehouses of strength and attainment.
—Henry Wood, Ideal Suggestion
Through Mental Photography, 1893

As a cat watching for mice does not look up though an elephant goes by, so they [people] are so busy mousing for defects that they let great excellences pass them unnoticed.
—The Banner of Light,
June 25, 1870

Past thought has limited us in all directions. We have tethered ourselves to a self-imposed post by imaginary cords.
—Henry Wood, *Ideal Suggestion Through Mental Photography*, 1893

Be filled with a pure and lofty aim, and when opposition comes, the soul's forces will gather and accumulate, and finally bust forth in a power like a thunderbolt, sweeping a clear path to success.
—*New England Spiritualist*, August 9, 1856

There is a dawning of a new period in the world's history. Let us stand firm for right and march to the front.
—*A Fountain of Light*, vol. 1, no. 26, 1881

HORACE GREELEY

No real satisfaction comes from
work done exclusively for self.
—*The World's Advance-Thought*,
no. 9, 1890

We must have co-operation, or we cannot
have power; supervision or we cannot
have order and security; organization
or we cannot have progression.
—*The Harbinger of Light*,
August 1, 1874

Believe that every hour, every moment of work
well done, makes up the treasure with which
success in the affairs of people is to be purchased.
—*The Spiritual Clarion*,
January 14, 1860

Let us seek knowledge, wisdom
and understanding; be diligent and
improve every opportunity.
—*A Fountain of Light*,
vol. 1, no. 3, 1890

The wisest of people have been of the opinion
that self-control is the true secret of success.
—THE TEMPLE MESSENGER,
OCTOBER 1890

When passion enters the front gate,
wisdom goes out the back.
—THE UNIVERCOELUM AND SPIRITUAL
PHILOSOPHER, MARCH 10, 1849

When governing others, you must do what
you can do, not all you would do.
—THE BANNER OF LIGHT,
MAY 7, 1859

Freedom is obedience. A bridge can
be built to stand but only in obedience
to the laws of mechanics.
—ANNIE PAYSON CALL, POWER
THROUGH REPOSE, 1891

Under all circumstances, keep an even mind.
—Andrew Jackson Davis,
The Magic Staff, 1857

The secret of happiness consists in removing unnecessary friction in one's own pathway and assisting to remove it from the pathways of others.
—Andrew Jackson Davis, Free Thoughts Concerning Religion; or Nature Versus Theology, c.1872

Nothing is attainable unless we love it.
—A Fountain of Light,
vol. 1, no. 1, 1880

We should so live and labor in our times that what came to us as seed may go to the next generation as blossom, and what came to as blossom, may go to them as fruit.
—Henry Ward Beecher, quoted in The Carrier Dove, April 14, 1888

Ambition is earthly, aspiration is spiritual.
—Andrew Jackson Davis, *The Harmonial Philosphy*, 1847

Intellectual laziness is a greater bar to prosperity than physical laziness.
—*The World's Advance-Thought*, no. 11, 1890

Industry is what warrants success.
—*The Agitator*, June 1, 1858

We can sometimes love that which we do not understand, but it is impossible clearly to understand what we do not love.
—*A Fountain of Light*, vol. 1, no. 7, 1880

Fame should be the consequence—not the motive—of our actions.
—*The Temple Messenger*, September 1890

Duties in general, like that class of things called debts, give more trouble the longer they remain undischarged.
—*Age of Progress*, November 25, 1854

One snowflake is a very small, weak thing. So is one ballot. But when snowflakes unite and co-operate they can overcome steam, stop the Lightning Express, and paralyze a great metropolis. Ballots united and falling from the hand of intelligence and morality into the ballot box can make people free.
—*The Carrier Dove*, June 2, 1888, quoting *The Industrial News*

When public officials are forced to realize that they are the servants, not the masters of the people, there will be no further opportunity for over-reaching on the part of anyone.
—*The Banner of Light*, December 3, 1898

Frank Haddock

Frank Haddock was an example of character in the 19th century. He was born in Watertown, New York, in 1853. His father was a minister and an opponent of Spiritualism, but also an opponent of slavery and unpaid prison labor. When he was a child, upon returning to his home after running away, his father said, "Hello, Frank, you got back! You'll probably want some supper!"

Frank Haddock became an orator. He married in 1877 and by 1882 was admitted to the Wisconsin bar. Like his father, he became an ordained minister. He believed that it was in the training of the will (character) that we could cultivate our personalities.

By writing several books, including *The Power of Will*, *Power for Success* and *Practical Psychology*, Frank Haddock showed that it is possible with hard work and determination to develop character. Although not considered part of the Spiritualists, he was part of the "New Thought/Mental Healing" movement. His books have been used to train generations of spiritualists.

His final book, *Creative Personality*, was published after he died.

Character

A worthy person, by their very presence, promises us much.
—*The Radical Spiritualist*,
April 1860

Care not so much for your reputation as for your character—the former is only what the world thinks of you while the latter is what you really are.
—*New England Spiritualist*,
August 22, 1857

Long has materialism reigned over the minds of people; and beneath its chilling power the fairest flowers of hope and joy have been withered.
—*The Spirit Messenger*,
October 16, 1852

A true and pure character is more to be
desired than wealth, gold and diamonds.
—A FOUNTAIN OF LIGHT,
VOL.1, NO. 23, 1881

The body is a grand composite photograph
of previous thinking and mental states.
—HENRY WOOD, IDEAL SUGGESTION
THROUGH MENTAL PHOTOGRAPHY, 1893

One reason that the world is not reformed is
because every person that is bent on reforming
others does not think of reforming themselves.
—THE BANNER OF LIGHT,
OCTOBER 5, 1870

Intellectual wealth is a grand thing,
but moral affluence is grander.
—THE CARRIER DOVE,
JANUARY 1886

It is easy in the world to live after the world's opinion; it is easy in solitude to live after your own; but the great person is one who in the midst of the crowd keeps with perfect sweetness the independence of solitude.
—THE AGITATOR,
AUGUST 1, 1858

You cannot dream yourself into a character; you must hammer and forge yourself one.
—THE BANNER OF LIGHT,
FEBRUARY 19, 1880

Good people are human suns! They brighten and warm whatever they pass.
—NEW ENGLAND SPIRITUALIST,
FEBRUARY 14, 1857

Laziness promises a person ease for the present, which is sure to produce a terrible future—therefore resist laziness as you would the devil.
—A FOUNTAIN OF LIGHT,
VOL. 1, NO. 16, 1881

It is always good to know, if only in passing,
a charming human being; it refreshes one
like flowers and woods and clear brooks.
—*The Carrier Dove*,
June 2, 1888

A positively developed spiritual nature
is invulnerable to any evil.
—Henry Wood, *Ideal Suggestion
Through Mental Photography*, 1893

Self-conquest is the greatest of all conquests.
—*New England Spiritualist*,
June 30, 1855

Self-control lies at the foundation of
character. A person who does not control
themselves must be controlled by others.
—*The Carrier Dove*,
June 2, 1888

Happiness comes from within, not without.
—THE BANNER OF LIGHT,
JANUARY 8, 1870

The mortals who neglect their earthly duties to seek the celestial are like one who would keep their eyes continually on the noonday sun. The dazzling light would only serve to find them, and they would neither see the beauty around them nor the pitfalls they are liable to tumble onto.
—THE WORLD'S ADVANCE-THOUGHT,
NO. 22, 1890

To patronize humanity is not to love humanity.
—THE UNIVERSAL REPUBLIC,
NO. 9, 1890

If the sunshine could be hoarded and locked up like gold, the earth would soon be left in darkness.
—THE WORLD'S ADVANCE-THOUGHT, 1890

The person who does the most, has the least time to talk about what they do.
—*New England Spiritualist*,
March 28, 1857

Purity is not with creeds, but with individuals.
—*A Fountain of Light*,
vol. 1, no. 6, 1880

No reputation can be permanent that does not spring from principle.
—*The Radical Spiritualist*,
October 1859

Every move on the chessboard of life that gives you more power brings with it higher responsibility.
—*The Philosophical Journal/ The Religio-Philosophical Journal*,
October 14, 1865

A kind and generous spirit, carried through every work, is a living example—a sermon—let us preach such sermons every day.
—*A Fountain of Light*,
vol. 1, no. 17, 1881

The serpent that tempted Eve was said to be a living one; but the modern serpent that tempts men and women is made of gold.
—*The World's Advance-Thought*,
no. 3, 1890

Only they who would not be a despot are free to be a freeman.
—*The Universal Republic*,
no. 9, 1890

Convicts are reflections of criminals in high power.
—*The World's Advance-Thought/ The Universal Republic*, no. 9, 1890

Material property without spiritual growth is more a cause for regret than Thanksgiving.
—*The World's Advance-Thought*, no. 3, 1890

The person who loses conscience has nothing left worth keeping.
—*The Spiritual Clarion*, May 9, 1857

Lies are like swords that can cut the hands that wield them.
—*New England Spiritualist*, August 1, 1857

The ordinary person confesses their faults; great people feel them.
—*The Radical Spiritualist*, November 11, 1859

It is a waste of time to complain of
other people's faults. The best thing
we can do is mend our own.
—The Univercoelum and Spiritual
Philosopher, January 20, 1849

If the wants of the poor are ever to be alleviated,
people must turn their gaze from heaven to earth.
—Truth Seeker,
March 23, 1883

People's inhumanity to others makes
countless millions mourn.
—Shekinah, 1852

Inspired thoughts of living people are
like stars at the celestial gates.
—S.B. Bitten in The Spiritual
Clarion, January 14, 1860

Neither the monopolization of ideas nor material wealth comprehends universality—for the former would restrict all intellectual power to their individual mind, and the latter would restrict all material riches to their person.
—*The World's Advance-Thought,*
no. 3, 1890

Lying is the consummate form of cowardice.
—*The Univercoelum and Spiritual Philosopher,* March 10, 1849

If a person fails to the amount of millions it is all right, but let a person fail in a month of their board bill [rent] and that person is considered a rascal.
—*The Radical Spiritualist,*
June 1858

E.W. AND M.H. WALLIS

There are many mediums in Spiritualism, but rarely do we see a couple who has worked together, written together and lectured together. The Wallis's did all of that. They are most well known for their book, *A Guide to Mediumship and Psychic Unfoldment*.

Working together, they exhibited the true power of love. E.M. Wallis was from a family that had mediumistic talent. When Mrs. Wallis (M.H. Wallis) was seventeen, she and her mother went to live with Spiritualists. The community they lived in felt that she had talent as a medium. She met E.W. Wallis in 1875 at the Spiritual Institution and they were married shortly after.

Together they toured America and England, living a Spiritualist life, writing and lecturing. They had children and said more than once that their children were carried across the room by materialized spirits.

If there was conflict in their relationship, we do not know of it; we know only of their love and productivity.

Their work and love for each other is an inspiration to us all.

Love

Nothing is more beautiful and divine on earth than the aspiration of a loving heart, and the breathings of a free spirit.
—*The Spirit Messenger*,
December 14, 1850

Love feels no load.
—*Banner of Light*,
February 10, 1849

A wife or husband's love is better than a sweetheart's.
—*The Banner of Light*,
July 30, 1870

Those who have sensed their friend's superiority have ceased to love that friend.
—*The Banner of Light*,
April 2, 1880

Do not keep the alabaster boxes of your love and tenderness shut up until your friends are dead. Fill their lives with sweetness. Speak approving, cheering words while their ears can hear them and their hearts be thrilled by them. The things you mean to say when they are gone, say before they go.
—*A Fountain of Light*,
vol. 1, no. 27, 1881

No one can be wise without love, and no one can truly love and not be wise.
—James J. Owen,
Spiritual Fragments, 1890

Love, will and wisdom are the fundamental elements of human nature.
—*The Univercoelum and Spiritual Philosopher*, January 6, 1849

When all other weapons fall, love will conquer.
—The Radical Spiritualist,
December 1859

Go slowly to the entertainment of friends,
but quickly to their misfortunes.
—The Spirit Messenger,
April 9, 1853

Love is the primary cause of all phenomena in physical creation. Love is the soul of the Deity.
—Andrew Jackson Davis, The Great Harmonia: The Teacher, vol. 2, 1875

Gratitude is the music of the heart when its cords are swept away by the gentle breeze of kindness.
—The Banner of Light,
February 19, 1870

Love is the impelling force that carries us forward on the road of progress. Hatred clogs our way and holds us back.
—*The World's Advance-Thought*, no. 3, 1880

When other means fail, remember that a word spoken in love, even a tear or a smile, may reclaim the wanderer.
—*The Univercoelum and Spiritual Philosopher*, December 4, 1847

A good thought reverberates through the spheres of love and wisdom, making glad the hearts of angels.
—*The Harbinger of Light*, October 1, 1870

A faithful friend is one who will give me one loaf when they have but two.
—*Age of Progress*, October 7, 1854

The Life of everything is love, but the form of love, the shape in which love appears is determined by wisdom.
—THE FRIEND OF PROGRESS,
MAY 1859

A person would rather have good company in the desert than be alone in paradise.
—THE UNIVERCOELUM AND SPIRITUAL PHILOSOPHER, FEBRUARY 10, 1849

The more we love others, the more our capacity to love increases.
—A FOUNTAIN OF LIGHT,
VOL. 1, NO. 7, 1880

No person loves their brother or sister when they wish to get ahead of them.
—THE WORLD'S ADVANCE-THOUGHT,
NO. 11, 1890

Love is the fulfilling of law.
—*Kingdom of Heaven*,
January 1874

A loving heart and pleasant disposition are commodities a person should never fail to take home with them.
—*The Banner of Light*,
July 16, 1870

God cannot purchase a treasure so precious as a person's love. Time cannot mar its beauty; distance but strengthens its influence.
—*A Fountain of Light*,
vol. 1, no. 11, 1880

Strange that hearts can live on after breaking.
—*The Banner of Light*,
January 16, 1864

Society has been compared to a heap of embers, which when parted soon languish, darken, expire; but if placed together, glow with ruddy and intense heat.
—*The Univercoelum and Spiritual Philosopher*, March 10, 1849

Love is the source of quantity in a person. There is great fullness of life where there is great affection, which flows out of love's foundation.
—Andrew Jackson Davis, *Views of Our Heavenly Home*, 1878

There is a vast deal of vital air in loving words.
—*The Spiritual Clarion*, May 9, 1857

The love of others as surely brings happiness with it as heat brings warmth.
—*A Fountain of Light*, vol.1, no. 7, 1880

People grow in wisdom and love as they grow
in purity and strength. Spiritual strength is,
as body strength, increased by exercise.
—*Friends of Progress*,
December 1864

Love and peace are twins. Where love
abounds, peace and good will to all
is carried out in daily practice.
—*A Fountain of Light*,
vol. 1, no. 13, 1880

Love is life, and blame and hate are death.
—*Kingdom of Heaven*,
January 1874

Soon as intelligence sparkles in the eye,
love also shows its light.
—*Friends of Progress*,
May 1865

There is not one human being in a million,
whose stony heart can withstand
the power of love.
—The Philosophical Journal/
The Religio-Philosophical
Journal, October 7, 1865

To love is to live; to hate is to die.
—The World's Advance-Thought,
no. 11, 1890

Dear to us who love us,
they enlarge our lives.
—The Radical Spiritualist,
March 1860

Cora Wilburn

A popular Spiritualist writer, Cora Wilburn was originally of the Jewish faith who converted to Spiritualism in search of what she considered a more loving God. Although she was born into a wealthy Southern family, her parents died when she was a child, leaving Wilburn a penniless orphan.

Left on her own to survive, Cora Wilburn sewed for others to make a living. Of this time in her life, Cora Wilburn wrote, "I was a toiler at my needle . . . I had been a dweller in the sunny Southern climates, unaccustomed to labor of any kind; an only child and a spoiled one. Who aided me in my investigation of my own soul's destiny? God's ministering spirits did."

Wilburn's greatest impact came through her writings. She wrote a series of articles titled "My Religion." She spoke fluent German and often translated articles for *The Banner of Light*. She was popular for her poetry and fiction and she used both to promote women's rights.

She is known for her book of poetry, *The Spiritual Significance of Gems*.

Experience

It is well to learn from the experience of others.
—FRIENDS OF PROGRESS,
AUGUST 1865

Inner experiences are so silent they go unperceived and unknown. They make their appearance on the surface but very often, even if observed, they are not inquired about.
—THE BANNER OF LIGHT,
SEPTEMBER 24, 1857

Whenever a new view of life presents itself to the soul, taking captive the thought, seizing hold of the faith, and creating an entirely new philosophy by which to shape and direct actions—that is a new experience, and a deep one, because it cannot fail to be lasting.
—THE BANNER OF LIGHT,
SEPTEMBER 24, 1857

We learn by experience lessons of wisdom, of patience, of hope and truth. We also learn lessons of sorrow and grief, but they all make up life. Let us not forget our blessings and mercies, as we remember our misfortunes.
—*A Foundation of Life*,
vol. 1, no. 15, 1881

To most people, experience is like the stern lights of a ship that illuminates only the track it has passed.
—*The Banner of Light*,
April 25, 1857

One who lives from within and seeks to apply every experience in such a manner as to develop their soul, it is such a man or woman who is ever able to make the bitterest disappointments of life the grander of triumphs in the realm of the soul.
—*The Banner of Light*,
October 22, 1898

Experience teaches us that there is only one road to happiness—fulfillment of duty.
—*The Banner of Light*,
January 8, 1891

The riches of experience are strewn all over the highway of human progress.
—Andrew Jackson Davis,
The Present Age and Inner Life, 1853

Past experience is well to think upon, but present experience is better to act upon.
—*The Spirit Messenger*,
November 6, 1852

Notes on the Sources Used

We began our search with the holdings of the National Spiritualist Association and The Marion Skidmore library in Lily Dale, New York, in 1990, accessing their many books and journals. We also have spent time at Harvard University's Widener Library, the Library of Congress and at The American Antiquarian Society in Worcester, Massachusetts.

In addition, we met Ann Braude, and she came to Lily Dale. She has read the entire Banner of Light, and is well known for her survey of the periodicals, *News from the Spirit World: A Checklist of American Spiritualist Periodicals, 1847–1900*. We received an estimate from Harvard about digitizing the Banner of Light so it could be read on line, however a wonderful organization, IAPSOP (The International Organization for the Preservation of Spiritualist and Occult Periodicals), now has many of the oldest Spiritual newspapers online. It is a wonderful thing to be able to sit in your living room and read them, as opposed to finding a parking space in Cambridge, Massachusetts.

Through the work of Pat Deveney, IAPOSP has been able to find the actual publication dates from beginning to end of many of the newspapers we quoted. There are still newspapers lost to time, but perhaps with people knowing more and reading more, the older "lost" newspapers and periodicals will turn up.

The following is a summary of what we know exists in terms of these periodicals and newspapers, mostly from the database of Pat Deveney and IAPOSP:

Age of Progress:
Devoted to the Development and Propagation of Truth, the Enfranchisement and Cultivation of the Human Mind. 1854–1858, weekly, Buffalo, NY.

Agitator, The.
A Semi-Monthly Journal of Reform / Devoted to Reform. 1858–1860 Monthly, then semi-monthly, Cleveland, OH.

Banner of Light, The.
A Weekly Journal of Romance Literature and General Intelligence / An Exponent of the Spiritual Philosophy of the Nineteenth/Twentieth Century. 1857–1907 weekly, and then monthly in last issue (1907) Boston, MA, except for a very short period in New York, NY, in 1859. This is the longest-running Spiritualist newspaper known.

Carrier Dove, The.
An Illustrated Weekly Journal Devoted to Spiritualism and Reform. 1883–1893 Monthly until 1887, weekly until 1889, then monthly. Oakland, CA, then San Francisco, CA, then Oakland, CA.

Fountain of Light, A.
A Weekly Journal, devoted to Light Seekers. 1880–1881 Weekly. Quincy, IL.

NOTES ON THE SOURCES USED

Free Thought Magazine.
1882–1894. Monthly and then bimonthly. Buffalo, and Salamanca, NY, and in 1895 in Chicago, IL.

Friend of Progress, The.
1864–1865 Monthly. New York, NY.

Golden Way, The.
1891 Monthly. San Francisco: CA. Succeeds: The Golden Gate, April 1891–October 1891.

Harbinger of Light, The.
A monthly journal devoted to Zoistic Science, free thought, Spiritualism and the Harmonial philosophy. A monthly journal devoted to psychology, Occultism, and spiritual philosophy. 1870 to 1954 Monthly. Melbourne, Victoria, Australia.

Kingdom of Heaven, The.
On Earth peace, good will toward men. 1864–1875 Monthly. Anderson, IN, Huntsville, IN, Berlin Heights, OH, Syracuse, NY, Boston, MA.

New England Spiritualist.
A Journal of the Methods and Philosophy of Spirit-Manifestation, and its Uses to Mankind. Light! More Light Still!—Goethe. 1855–1857 Weekly. Boston, MA.

Radical Spiritualist, The.
Truth, Love, Wisdom / No Union with Warriors. 1859–1860 Monthly. Hopedale (Milford), MA. "Free to the Outcast; to the Able and Willing, 50 cts. a year in Advance."

Religio-Philosophical Journal, The.
Devoted to Spiritual Philosophy / Truth Wears no Mask, bows at no Human Shrine, Seeks Neither Place nor Applause: She Only Asks a Hearing / Devoted to Spiritual Philosophy, Rational Religion and Psychical Research.

Other titles: The Philosophical Journal / The Religio-Philosophical Journal and Weekly Occult News. 1865–1905 Weekly. Chicago, IL, then at the turn of the Century, San Francisco, CA.

Shekinah, The.
Devoted to the Emancipation of Mind, the Elucidation of Vital, Mental, and Spiritual Phemonena, and the Progress of Man. 1851–1853 Quarterly, then every other month, then monthly. Bridgeport, CT, and then New York, NY. Publisher: S.B. Brittan Succeeded by: Buchanan's Journal of Man

Spiritual Clarion, The.
The Facts, Philosophy, Religion, Reform and Freedom of Spiritualism / Spiritualism, its Tests, Harmony, Philosophy and Religion / A Journal of Distinctive and Harmonic Spiritualism. 1856–1860 Weekly, then semimonthly, then monthly.

Auburn, NY—With volume two (August 9, 1851) the journal changed its title to The Spirit Messenger and Harmonial Guide, and in October 1851 moved its offices to New York, NY.

Spiritual Telegraph, The.
Devoted to the Illustration of Spiritual Intercourse. The Agitation of Thought is the Beginning of Wisdom.

Other titles: Spiritual Telegraph and Fireside Preacher (beginning May 1, 1858). 1852–1859 Weekly. New York, NY.

NOTES ON THE SOURCES USED

Temple Messenger, The.
There are only two known issues of The Temple Messenger, both in 1890. It was the written organ of the Spiritualist Church and was then on the corner of Newbury and Exeter Street in Boston, MA. It later became the Exeter Street Theater and then a store.

Truthseeker.
Devoted to Science, Morals, Free Thought, Free Enquiry and the Diffusion of Liberal Sentiments. 1873 Monthly through 1875; weekly then through 1929; then semimonthly. Paris, IL, then New York, NY; San Diego, CA. Publisher: Liberal Association of Paris,

Univercoelum and Spiritual Philosopher, The.
The Things which are Seen are Temporal, but the Things which are Not Seen are Eternal. 1847–1849 Weekly. New York, NY.

Voice of Angels.
January 1878–December 15, 1880, twice monthly. North Weymouth, MA.

World's Advance-Thought, The, and **The Universal Republic.**
A Spirited Monthly Newspaper, Devoted to Advanced Spiritual Ideas / Avant-Courier of the New Spiritual Dispensation / Love is the Way, the Truth and the Light / An Advocate of Spiritualism. Truths of all Religions Given Expression.
1886–1918 Monthly. Salem then Portland, OR, and then Portland, OR, and London, England.

Books Used for Quotations

Call, Annie Payson. *Power Through Repose.* N.p.:Roberts Brothers, 1891. Little, Brown and Company, 1900. [Available online at no cost via www.archive.org]

Davis, Della E., M.D., ed. *Starnos: Quotations from the inspired writings of Andrew Jackson Davis.* Boston: Colby & Rich. 1891. Andrew Jackson Davis began his work before the Hydesville rappings in 1848. After his work in Mesmerism (hypnotism) and most of his writing of books—said to be thirty of them—he went to medical school where he met his last wife, Della Davis. From his books, she selected and edited this book of his quotes. It is in the public domain and available at no cost online via https://www.archive.org

Denton, William and Elizabeth M. F. Denton *The Soul Of Things: or, Psychometric Researches and Discoveries.* Boston: Walker, Wise and Company, 1863. [Available at no cost online via www.archive.org]

Holmes, Alfred I. *Life Thoughts from Pulpits and From Poets.* Brooklyn, NY: Published by the author, 1872.

Newcomb, Katharine H. *Helps to Right Living.* Boston: Lee and Shepard, 1899.

Owen, James J. *Spiritual Fragments.* San Francisco: The Rosental-Saalburg Co., 1890. [Available online at no cost via www.archive.org]

Wood, Henry. *Ideal Suggestion Through Mental Photography.* Boston: Lee and Shepard, 1893.

Acknowledgments

First and foremost, we would like to thank Professor Cathy Smith. Many years ago she had the idea of quotes paired with short bios. She helped us with the initial writing and found people such as Dr. Valmour, whom we would never have found without her help.

We also want to thank Ann Braude for her amazing work over the years. No modern historian has accomplished what she has.

Our thanks to the library at Lily Dale Assembly, known as the Marion Skidmore Library; the NSA office and Library at Lily Dale; the Harvard University Widener Library; the Antiquarian Society in Worcester, Massachusetts; as well as The Library of Congress. We spent many hours in these places before so many holdings were put on the Internet. A huge thank you to The International Association for the Preservation for Spiritualist and Occult Periodicals (IAPSOP) for taking on a monumental job that we could only imagine and putting most of this material online.

19TH CENTURY QUOTES FOR 21ST CENTURY LIVING

We would both like to thank the ministers of the Church of the Living Spirit, who provide guidance throughout the year: they are all Reverends! Rose Clifford, Brenda Freay-Holl, John Gordon, Rhonda Hoadley, Sharon Klinger, E. Gerta Lestock, Sharon Pieri, Patricia Price, Judith Rochester, MK Gadeke Roland, Alexis Rolnick, Jewel Rozanski, Dr. Neal Rzepkowski, Colleen Vanderzyden, and Lisa Williams.

Anna Donovan is deeply thankful for the support of her family. Her parents, Al and Del, who are gone but with her every day of her life. Her husband, Joe. Her children, Sara and Danny, and their spouses, David and Kim. And her biggest cheerleader, Anna's sister-cousin Elaine Brabson in Tennessee.

Chancellor Charles Modica and his wife, Lisa, of St. George's University in Grenada are champions for everyone's endeavors. We would like to acknowledge Drs. Satesh Bidaisee, Joseph Childers, Joseph Feldman, Calum Macpherson and Cheryl Cox Macpherson, C.V. Rao, Trevor Noel , Daniel Ricciardi, Randall Waechter, as well as Julie Babka, Anthia Parke, and Jonathan Modica, and Andrew Sheiner.

A good portion of this book was written in the Fox News Channel Bureau's green room in Washington, D.C., while Ellen Ratner waited to go on air. It is because of this quiet space and time for reflection that this book could be written. The coffee, company, and comfort was great. We would like to thank Marilisa Battistella, Shari Berger, Melissa Chisel, Debi deFrank, Nicole Ferguson, Cathy Kades, Rachelle Lorick, Tamara Montgomery, Rosetta Murry, Renata Nippy-Kelly, Carley Pressley, and Brooke Smith. Also, those on the booking desk: Kaitlyn Chamberlin, Brian Doherty, Bridget Mary Mcdonnell, Erenia Michell,

ACKNOWLEDGMENTS

Elise Norris, Cherie Paquette, Christina Robbins, and Caroline Whiteman. And it is always a joy to see Walter Carter.

Also from Fox News Channel, Suzanne Scott, Dianne Brandi, Chris Snyder, Mitch Davis, and Jack Abernethy—our thanks to all of you for years of friendship and support; and, of course, producer Patricia Peart. In addition, Don Grannum and Christina Cassese are always helpful and friendly. From Fox's .com, we would like to thank: Justin Craig, Kevin Tracy, Molly Dodd, Avi Ramsadeen. Emily DeCiccio, and, of course, Lynne Jordal Martin who has vision as well as editorial insight!

In the Los Angeles Bureau, there are several people who always make the wait productive and worthwhile. They are Jamie Brennan, Melissa Chrise, Connie Cole, Gigi deLeon, Kristin Durante, Don Fair, Dan Gallo, Jen Girdon, Kelly Greer, Nancy Harmeyer, Richard Hernandez, Adam Housley, Cathy James, Blanche Johnson, Jessica Miller, Laura Prabucki, Corbett Riner, Lee Ross, Michael Setsuda, Matt Sawicki, and Gene Stratton.

Ellen would like to especially thank the folks at RMS who came to her ordination: Cindy Cuffaro, Candi Johnson, Nora Breznai, Mark Tepsich, and, of course, RMS Director Bruce Geier.

Thank you family and friends who also came: Gabrielle Miller, Tawny Ratner, Lorri Webb, and Cathy Smith.

Karyl Andosca, Amy Johnson, and Ida Berkobein have been to Lily Dale with support and love.

We would also like to thank: Darrianne Bramberg, Jon Christopher Bua, Ed Butowsky, Jay Byrne, Diana Cepeda, John Chang, Greg Clugston, Mike Collins, Shelly Kapoor Collins, George Condon, Brian Doyle, Justin Duckham, Ellen Eckert, Sharon

Edwards, Lovisa Frost, Diane Gooch, Dr. Bryna J. Harwood, Kinsey Harvey, Scott Hoganson, Geoff Holtzman, Martha Hood, Victoria Jones, Peter and Blanche Johnson, Dr. Chatchai Kokar, Olga Ramirez Kornacki, Martha Kumar, Michael Lawrence, Loree Lewis, Terry Lierman, Julie Lule, Dr. Rupa Iyengar, Timothy Maier, Mike Mastrian, Bianca McDown, Nancy Fraser Michalski and Rich Michalski, Judy Miller, Jasia Miszkiel, Sadie Mitnick, Audrey Mullen, former Congressman Bob Ney, Shantrell Nicks, Darrin Peterson, Jim and Elizabeth Pinkerton, Mark Pfeifle, Scott Reber, Jack Rice, William Richardson, lawyer Richard Robinson, lawyer Michele Ross, April Ryan, Naratom Sayal, Tony Sayegh, Bill and Darla Shine, my cousin Joyce Singer, Rob Skinner, Pamela Stevens, Kandi Stroud, Dr. Zsofia Szabo, Jay Tamboli, Luke Vargas, Danielle Vignjevich, and our many, many interns.

Sean Spicer, who has always been so kind to everyone.

When he was on the planet, Dr. Eugene Taylor was a terrific teacher and guide.

Ellen's biological family and in-laws are Ellen's other support system. Her late brother, Michael; brother, Bruce; cousins Albert and Audrey Ratner; James and Susan Ratner, Charles and Ilana Horowitz Ratner, Mark and Nancy Ratner, Ronald and Rebecca Ratner, Paula Krulak, Joan Shafran and Rob Haimes, Charlotte Haynes, Karen Ranucci; Lizzy, Rebbie, Patrick, Ana, Jake, Elias, and Elana Stein; Tony DiLella; Chip, Lisa, Chase and Karen, Chance, Chandler and Charli Espinoza; Valerie Espinoza; James Johnson; Dr. Pamela Lipkin and Michael Carajohn, Julie Ratner and Sam Eskenazi; Kate Taylor and Linda McCarthy.

We can't forget the people who labor everyday on radio. Like the old-time Spiritualists, they tell people what they feel and the news of the day—even if it is not pleasant. We would like to thank our radio family. People, it is always a pleasure having you in our sphere: Marc Bernier, Steve Bowers, Kate Delaney, Earle Farrell, Mark Grimaldi, Thom and Louise Hartmann, Keith Hansen Jack Heath, Scott Hennen, George Hook, Chris Lenois, Tony Lopes, Leslie Marshall, Stan Milam, Dan Mitchell, Howard Monroe, Phil Paleologos, Ken Pittman, George Russell, Keith Shirley, Tom Shattuck, Rick Smith, Scott Thompson, Lisa Wexler, Fred Weinberg, Edward Woodson.

From the Lily Dale Community we would like to thank Cori Lynn Augustine and Brad Thomas Bettis and their company, Making Things Beautiful, as well as Susan Glasier from Lily Dale office. As we were reading the newspapers and books from the 19th century, we cannot forget the guidance provided by Rev. B. Anne Gehman. She and her daughter Rhonda St. Amant are the very best teachers and counselors.

Shari Johnson is the world's best editor! Thank you! Thanks also to Gary Rosenberg of TheBookCouple for his design and production.

Finally, Dr. Cholene Espinoza, who used to think of Spiritualism as crazy and odd, and who has now come around!

Index

abolition, 93–94
abuse, domestic, 100
accomplishments, 114–123
accusations, 42
actions, 31, 32, 33, 90, 104, 109, 110, 115, 121, 122, 130, 148
    toward others, 41, 42, 43, 44, 45, 51, 53, 100, 133, 141
adversity, 70–74, 95, 96
advice-giving, 12
afflictions, 71, 72, 74, 95, 96
age and aging, 59, 71, 87, 91, 109
ambition, 122
angels, 86
art, 116
aspirations, 39, 100, 118, 122
attention, 31
Aversion, John B. *See* Valmour, Dr.

bankruptcy, 134
Baumfree, Isabella. *See* Truth, Sojourner
beauty, 59, 83
Beecher, Henry Ward, 35, 103, 121
behavior, , 84, 91, 99, 100, 102, 110

bigotry, 89, 106
Bitten, S.B., 133
blame, 43, 143
blessings, 106
Blood, James H., 75
body, physical, 13, 27, 66, 84
Bowditch, William I., 93
Braude, Ann, 2, 4
Britten, Emma Hardinge, 18–19, 29
Browning, Elizabeth Barrett, 35
Bruckner, Fannie, 47
Buckman, Ruben, 75

Call, Annie Payson, 13, 55, 84, 120
Carey, Alice, 49
Carter, Jeremiah, 97
cats, 11
Cercle Harmonique, 29–30
character, 44, 45, 90, 106, 109, 111, 115, 124, 125–134, 137
charisma, 117
charity, 51, 52, 53, 111
charm, 128
cheating, 86
cheerfulness, 34
Christianity, 89
church-going, 101

163

circumstances, 92
Civil War, 1–2, 82
Clafin, Roxanna, 75
Claflin, Tennessee Celeste, 75
Clark, Emily Suzanne, 29–30
cleanliness, 31
Colburn, Nellie, 68
colleges, 9
common good, 52, 92
common sense, 32
communication and words, 37–46, 50, 80, 109, 137
compassion, 54
competitiveness, 141
composure, 11
condemnation, 42, 102
condescension, 128
conduct. See behavior
confidence, 33, 114
Conklin, John, 68
conscience, 65, 83, 86, 99, 111, 132
consciousness, inner, 14, 104, 146
consideration, 41
contentment, 90
cooperation, 119
courage, 11, 95–96
cowardice, 134
creeds, 105, 106, 130
criticism, 42, 43, 44, 45, 46, 115, 133
crying, 139

Daggett, Melissa, 29
Davis, Andrew Jackson
  on accomplishment and governing/government, 117, 121, 122
  on communication and words, 46

on courage, 96
on experience, 148
on home and religion, 100, 103, 105, 107, 108, 109
on knowledge and wisdom, 13, 14, 15
on love, 138, 142
on spiritualism, 25, 26, 27, 28
on the soul, 64, 65, 66
on truth and living with yourself, 87, 88, 89, 91, 92, 95
on women and men, 78, 79
death, 21, 22, 25
debt, 134
deceit, 56, 86, 114
democracy, 38
Denton, Elizabeth M.F., 63, 64
Denton, William, 63, 64
desires, 85, 90, 91
despotism, 131
determination, 109
diet, 12, 34
diligence, 119
disappointments, 70, 147
discord, 20, 32, 45, 106, 121
discoveries, 34
disputes, 38, 45, 77
diversity, 33
divinity, 65, 103, 104, 110
dogma, 105
Douglas, Stephen, 68
Douglass, Frederick, 76, 94
Dr. Hedges (spirit), 97
drinking, 45, 53
duties, 31–34, 110, 123, 129, 148

Edmonds, John Worth, 7–8
education, 9, 13, 15, 79, 94
Emerson, Ralph Waldo, 85

INDEX

empathy, 48–56
enemies, 85
envy, 51
equality, 50, 81–82, 93
errors, 89, 91
evil, 73
expectations, 95
experience, 109, 146–148

faith, 89, 99, 105
fame, 122
faultfinding, 42, 43, 44, 115, 117, 133
faults, 46, 132, 133
favoritism, 50
feelings, 101
First Spiritualist Church, 47
fools, 9
Fox, John, 4
Fox, Margaret, 4
fraternity, 21
free love. *See* love, free
freedom, 50, 123, 131
freeloading, 114
friendship, 85, 136, 137, 138, 139, 140, 141, 143
future, 27, 54, 116

Garrison, William Lloyd, 93
generosity, 44, 50, 51, 53, 55, 131
glory, 44
God, 24, 25, 26, 28, 59, 63, 67, 98, 99, 100, 103, 104, 105, 138
goodness, 59, 83, 86, 89, 104, 106, 108, 127, 139, 143
gossip, 40, 43, 110
governing and government, 20, 114–123

grace, 48–56
gratitude, 49, 138
Greeley, Horace, 9, 112–113
Green, Joseph, 22
grief, 147
Grindon, L.H., 50
Guide to Mediumship and Psychic Unfoldment (Wallis), 135

Haddock, Frank, 124
happiness, 54, 60, 71, 74, 86, 88, 100, 121, 129, 142, 148
harmony, 64, 89, 102, 109
hatred, 139, 143, 144
health, 20
heartbreak, 142
Heaven, 24, 54, 100, 105
Holland, J.G., 34
Holmes, Alfred I., 86
Holmes, Oliver Wendell, 36
homes, 2, 28, 98–111
honesty, 99
Hooker, Isabella Beecher, 35
hope, 95, 147
humanitarianism, 106
humans, nature of, 96, 108, 137
hypnotism, 97

idealism, 41
ideas, 38, 134
ignorance, 9, 10, 11, 12, 65
illnesses, 91
imagination, 24, 41, 118
immortality, 3, 22, 25, 30, 61, 63, 66, 92, 101, 103, 104
impulses, 73
industriousness, 122
ingenuousness, 114
instincts, 95, 115
intuition, 61

165

Jackson, Rebecca Cox, 5, 57–58
jealousy, 51, 111, 136
joy, 101
judgment, 116
justice, 14, 29, 42, 50, 56, 85, 103, 107

kindness, 49, 54, 108, 131, 138
knowledge, 9–17, 49, 119, 122, 144

labor, 33, 34, 88, 114, 116, 119, 121
laziness, 122, 127
learning, 95, 101
Lee, Ann, 3
lies and lying, 54, 88, 132, 134
life, 16, 34, 43, 64, 65, 67, 73, 74, 87, 90, 91, 96, 99, 100, 101, 102, 109, 121, 147
Light, George W., 71
Lily Dale, New York, 97
Lincoln, Abraham, 68, 82
Lincoln, Mary Todd, 68–69
listening, 55
loquaciousness, 42, 46
love, 41, 55, 59, 78, 99, 101, 103, 104, 111, 121, 122, 129, 136–144
  familial, 28, 98, 100, 101, 102, 136, 141
  free, 76
Luminous Brotherhood (Clark), 29–30

madness, 65
malice, 40, 43, 45
marriage, 77, 78, 79
Martin, John B., 76

materialism, 21, 22, 61, 125, 132, 134
men, 77–80
mercy, 103
merits, 41
mind, 13, 62, 63, 87, 105, 109
money, 51, 115, 129, 131
motion, 84
mountains, 99
music, 32

nature, 14, 33, 37, 60, 83, 98, 99, 104, 105, 106, 107
Nell, William Cooper, 5, 93–94
New York Tribune, 112, 113
Newcomb, Katharine, 63, 67
niceness, 128

obedience, 120
open-mindedness, 121
opportunities, 114, 116, 119
orderliness, 108, 119
organization, 119
Owen, James J., 10, 49, 51, 60, 83, 87, 100, 114, 115, 137

pain, 16, 71, 72
parenthood, 84
passion, 120
past, 27, 148
patience, 111, 147
peace, 106, 117, 143
perfection, 100
Perot, Rebecca, 58
philosophers, 55
pleasure, 71
poetry, 38, 40, 41, 43
politics. *See* governing and government
postal service, 94

INDEX

poverty, 55, 133
power, 119, 130, 131
prayers, 62, 64, 101
preachers, 50
preparation, 95
present, 27, 116, 148
pride, 11
principles. *See* character
prisons, 8
progress, 110, 119, 121, 139, 148
prostitution, 46
purity, 130

qualifications, 116

Radical Spirits, Spiritualism, and Women's Rights in Nineteenth-Century America (Braude), 2, 4
rationality, 117, 121
reason, 16, 24
reformation, 3, 26, 102, 126
Reinhold, Ernest. *See* Britten, Emma Hardinge
relationships
   men and women, 77–80
   See also friendship; love
religion, 98–111
reputation, 125, 130
respect, 79
responsibility, 130
ridicule, 48
rights, human, 50, 118

sadness, 71
satisfaction, 91, 119
science, 89
Scott, Walter, 22
séances, 18, 29–30, 58, 68, 93, 113

seasons, 98
security, 119
self, 45, 60, 65, 67, 74, 83–90
self-control, 117, 120, 128
self-deception, 24
self-improvement, 39, 60
self-knowledge, 10, 11, 24, 25, 26, 32, 45, 59, 67, 84, 127, 147
selfishness, 13, 61, 88, 91, 119
Seneca Falls Convention, 4
senses, 23
Shakers, 3, 58
silence, 37, 40, 78
sinners, 52
sins, 52, 87
skill, 31–34
slander, 39, 40, 43, 110
slavery, 2, 4, 5, 81–82, 93–94
sleep, 64
smiling, 139
Smith, Sydney, 91
smoking, 86
society, 142
Society for the Diffusion of Spiritual Knowledge, 8
Socrates, 21
solitude, 62, 127
sorrows, 52, 63, 70, 71, 147
soul, 59–67, 83, 86, 96, 101, 103, 104, 109, 147
speech. *See* communication and words
speech, freedom of, 38, 50
Spirit Gifts (song), 3
spirit world, 136
   communication with, 3, 4, 29, 35, 47, 58, 65, 75, 97
Spiritualism, 5, 19, 20–28, 107
   beliefs, 2, 3, 25, 26, 27, 81, 93
   causes supported by, 4, 5

history of, 2–5, 18
newspapers, 5
spirituality, 12, 20, 22, 23, 24, 25, 27, 66, 88, 103, 104, 105, 128, 132, 143
stopping, 55
Stowe, Calvin, 35
Stowe, Harriet Beecher, 4–5, 35–36
Stowe, Henry, 35
success, 118, 119, 120, 122
suffering, 16, 52, 54, 71, 72, 85
supervision, 119
supportiveness, 137
Swedenborg, Emmanuel, 3
sympathy, 48, 55

talent, 31–34
talk. *See* communication and words
temper, 38
temperament, 141
temperance, 12
theology, 26, 98–111
thinking and thought, 10, 38, 44, 61, 62, 63, 95, 115, 117, 118, 122, 126, 133, 134
time, 101
timidity, 95
troubles. *See* afflictions
truth, 16, 24, 37, 46, 59, 60, 83–92, 147
Truth, Sojourner, 5, 81–82
Tuttle, Hudson, 32

understanding, 56, 119
universality, 134
universe, 100, 104
usefulness, 114

Valmour, Dr., 29
Vanderbilt, Cornelius, 75
virtues, 17, 72
voting, 123

Wallis, E.W., 135
Wallis, M.H., 135
war, 56, 117
Washington, George, 86
watching, 55
Way Memorial Temple, 47
wealth, 86, 115, 122, 131, 134
West, the, 112–113
whining, 53
wholesomeness, 117
Wilburn, Cora, 145
Wilcox, Ella Wheeler, 108
will. *See* character
wisdom, 9–17, 73, 89, 95, 119, 120, 126, 137, 139, 140, 143, 147
women, 77–80
women's rights, 2, 4, 5
Wood, Henry, 10, 24, 117, 118, 126, 128
Woodhull, Canning, 75
Woodhull, Victoria Claflin, 5, 75–76
Woodhull and Claflin's Weekly, 75–76
words. *See* communication and words
work. *See* labor
world, physical, 99, 100, 103, 104, 106, 107
worthiness, 14, 125

About the Authors

Ellen Ratner is an ordained Spiritualist minister at Church of the Living Spirit in Lily Dale, New York. She is also a media correspondent for Talk Media News, covering the White House and the United Nations.

Anna Donovan is a professional researcher in many different fields, including history and addictions.